Ludwig von Mises – a Primer

Ludwig von Mises – a Primer

EAMONN BUTLER

iea

The Institute of Economic Affairs

First published in Great Britain in 2010 by
The Institute of Economic Affairs
2 Lord North Street
Westminster
London SW1P 3LB
in association with Profile Books Ltd

The mission of the Institute of Economic Affairs is to improve public understanding of the fundamental institutions of a free society, by analysing and expounding the role of markets in solving economic and social problems.

A CIP catalogue record for this book is available from the British Library.

ISBN 978 0 255 36629 8

Many IEA publications are translated into languages other than English or are reprinted. Permission to translate or to reprint should be sought from the Director General at the address above.

Typeset in Stone by MacGuru Ltd
info@macguru.org.uk

Printed and bound in Great Britain by Hobbs the Printers

CONTENTS

THE AUTHOR

Dr Eamonn Butler is director of the Adam Smith Institute, an influential think thank that has designed policies to promote choice and competition in the delivery of essential services. He has degrees in economics, philosophy and psychology, gaining a PhD from the University of St Andrews in 1978. During the 1970s he also worked on pensions and welfare issues for the US House of Representatives, and taught philosophy in Hillsdale College, Michigan. On returning to the UK he served as editor of *The British Insurance Broker* before devoting himself full time to the Adam Smith Institute, which he helped found with his colleague Dr Madsen Pirie. Dr Butler is the author of books on the Nobel laureates Milton Friedman and F. A. Hayek, and author of *Ludwig von Mises: Fountainhead of the Modern Microeconomics Revolution*. For the IEA, he has authored *Adam Smith – a Primer*. He is also co-author of a number of books on intelligence and IQ testing, and a frequent contributor to UK print and broadcast media.

FOREWORD

When I left the Royal Air Force in 1999, entrepreneurial business was booming. By the time I completed my master's degree in computer science, it was over.

Why, I wondered, had everyone made the same mistake at once?

And so I discovered the Austrian Theory of the Trade Cycle and Ludwig von Mises. The credit crunch reinforced in my mind the value of the Austrian School and, in short order, a group of us established the Cobden Centre. The Centre was envisaged by Toby Baxendale to further the tradition of Manchester Liberalism and to provide a British home for the Austrian School of economics which would complement the more general work of the IEA in promoting various schools of free market thinking.

Though the intellectual chain was not continuous, Mises was perhaps the dominant author in a system of thinking that began in Salamanca in the fifteenth and sixteenth centuries among the Dominican and Jesuit scholastics who first wrote systematic treatises on economics. They knew, as Mises knew, that intervention in the mutual cooperation of free individuals was not reasonable or just. Price fixing in money, as in other commodities, is unwise and counterproductive, yet the central control of interest rates is just that: price fixing. Its fruit is our present crisis.

Mises's achievements are astonishing. Few people know that

F. A. Hayek was a socialist until he understood *Socialism: An Economic and Sociological Analysis*. People wrestle to reconcile individualism and society and yet Mises, a methodological individualist, wrote simply: 'Society is cooperation; it is community in action.'

How I wish every self-declared 'liberal' would read *Liberalism*, every banker *The Theory of Money and Credit*, every social scientist *Human Action* and every politician *Theory and History*. Mises is both neglected and misread by his critics: some truths are waiting to be rediscovered.

My particular choice among Mises's works is *Bureaucracy*. We learn that, for all the management styles and tools we may know, there are just two alternative categories of management: the private citizen's way and the government's way. That is, profit management or bureaucracy. Until we come to terms with profit as a measure of the value we have created for others and entrepreneurship as the creative search to help other people, our public services will languish: unhampered market prices are vital to rational economic calculation.

This is why Mises matters today: we appear to be living through his 'Crisis of Interventionism'. While we pile intervention upon intervention, it is increasingly apparent that our reserve of private wealth is becoming exhausted. Restrictive measures can only restrict output. Intervention in the market is demonstrably counterproductive: witness bonuses to staff at bailed-out banks which still fail to lend. Wealth is generated, not given, and present policies must eventually extinguish prosperity, security and freedom. What lies down this road is socialism of the German pattern, a present reality reported by David B. Smith in his IEA monograph *Living with Leviathan*.

The way out is not further intervention and the quality of countless lives depends on our discovering this fact. Over the last 100 years, public spending has risen inexorably from 10 to 15 per cent of factor-cost GDP to a forecast for 2010 of 53.4 per cent. We might reflect on what Mises wrote about the 'third way': 'The middle-of-the-road policy is not an economic system that can last. It is a method for the realization of socialism by instalments.'

Mises was a prolific author and in setting out to provide a representative primer, Eamonn Butler has attempted a giant task. He has succeeded magnificently in extracting the essence of Mises's thinking from thousands of pages of original work. I hope you enjoy this short book as much as I have. No academic would ever suggest to his students that they should not read the original works. As far as an introduction to Mises is concerned, however, Eamonn Butler's primer is superb: it will provide a valuable resource for all those setting out better to understand Mises's work.

STEVEN BAKER

Conservative prospective parliamentary candidate for Wycombe
Corporate Affairs Director, the Cobden Centre

February 2010

SUMMARY

- Economics is a science that can discover things and even make predictions – not on the basis of observation and testing, but through a process of *deduction*. Just as geometry or mathematics can be derived from a few simple and obvious axioms, so the science of human action can be deduced from the very concept of action and choice itself.
- Economic concepts such as cost and benefit are not *objective* but *subjective*, depending on the mind of the person involved. No amount of statistics can overcome the essential point that different people have different values, and that the response of one set of individuals to market events today may not be the same as others to events tomorrow. Values cannot be subjected to mathematical analysis.
- Profit is not just personal gain and it is not a measure of the happiness that we get from some successful action. Rather, profit encapsulates *other people's* valuation of what our initiative has contributed to *their* lives and welfare. It arises solely through the willing support of satisfied customers. In the market society, wealth is not a privilege, but comes only through benefiting consumers.
- The market system is much more efficient at allocating resources than political elections, where people get the opportunity to vote only every few years and have to choose

between packages of disparate policies. Every penny spent by consumers, in countless daily transactions, acts like a vote in a continual ballot, determining how much of each and every good should be produced and drawing production to where it is most urgently required.

- Free markets have no natural tendency to monopoly or monopoly prices; on the contrary, they have a powerful tendency towards diversity and differentiation, which bid quality up and prices down. Few cartels and monopolies would ever have come into being had it not been for government and the efforts of those with political power to stifle competition. Monopoly would be at its zenith under socialism, where all production is in state hands.

- Under socialism, production goods are held in common ownership. They are never traded, never bought and sold, but continue as joint property, so market prices are never established for them. Without prices and profits there is no efficient way of allocating resources. Decision-making becomes political and bureaucratic, leading to wasteful investment.

- Policies that are intended to 'improve' the market economy may in fact strangle it. Intervention may lead to unwelcome side effects that are then wrongly used to justify further interference, which in turn creates new problems, and so on. Eventually, although the economy still looks capitalist, it ends up being completely controlled by the authorities.

- The belief that state institutions can improve on the market by taking what it does and somehow doing it better is a dangerous conceit. In the absence of the profit motive, there is no obvious way of measuring the success of public agencies in delivering their objectives. Incentives for entrepreneurship are weak, and managers are likely to become risk-averse and bureaucratic.

- How we value time is an essential element in every action we take. Interest arises because people generally value present consumption more than future consumption. Postponing consumption to create capital goods is the route to increased wealth.

- Money is an economic good, but its purpose is neither production nor consumption. Its purpose is *exchange*. By printing money governments can create an artificial boom, but this must inevitably be followed by a bust. A painful adjustment process takes place as malinvestments are liquidated. A stable monetary system would have to be based on a commodity standard such as gold.

1 WHY MISES IS IMPORTANT

Ludwig von Mises (1881–1973) was one of the most significant economists and political scientists of the twentieth century. He became the leading figure of the 'Austrian School' of economics, which he consolidated and systematised.

Economists, he thought, must recognise that everything they deal with is rooted in the values and actions of human individuals. It is vain for economists to search, as natural scientists do, for mechanical linkages between measures like *aggregate demand* and *aggregate supply*, since these are mere statistics, which ignore the diversity of human beings and the values that motivate the economic life of those individuals. Rather, he maintained, economics is a deductive science: its principles can be derived logically from the very existence and nature of human purposes and actions.

Mises also argued that unhampered free markets were the only workable economic system. Socialism could not succeed because, without prices, it had no way of accurately calculating the costs of any action. He therefore regarded any government efforts to 'improve' the workings of the market economy as invariably destructive. Indeed, with his sweeping rejection of tariffs and subsidies, wage and price controls, restrictions over the free movement of goods and people, and state intrusion in the personal sphere, Mises set the standard for free market radicalism, laissez-faire politics, and thoroughgoing liberalism.[1]

When Mises became a Distinguished Fellow of the American Economic Association in 1969, he was credited as the author of nineteen books, many of them as large as they were seminal. Counting revised and foreign editions, the number reached 46. And since his death in 1973, at the age of 92, scores more translations, revisions and collections of his work have appeared.[2]

Intellectual contributions

It is invidious to select the most significant contributions from such a varied and extensive output. But six main headings may serve to show the width and depth of his intellectual achievements.

Economics is about individuals

First, Mises developed and systematised an approach to economics known as *subjectivism*. This holds that, to understand economics properly, we must trace it back to the actions and motives of *individuals* as they make choices, and buy, and sell.

Mainstream economists talk of how one macroeconomic variable (the *price level*, say) affects another (such as *aggregate demand*). But, says Mises, this overlooks the very thing that drives the whole system – the motives and actions of the individual human beings concerned. In fact there is no such thing as the

---

1   'Liberalism' is used here as Mises used it, in the European sense of personal freedom and limited government.

2   For a fuller account of his life and work, see E. Butler, *Ludwig von Mises: Fountainhead of the Modern Microeconomics Revolution*, Gower, Brookfield, VT, and Aldershot, 1988.

'price level' – prices in a market do not all rise and fall together, like the level of water in a bath. On the contrary, there are millions of individual prices, all changing up and down from moment to moment. It is hard to imagine that you could ever capture and record all these prices at some instant, or that compiling some average of them would do you any good: in the next instant they would all have changed again. Likewise, *demand* is the volume of particular goods that people choose to purchase – adding up the quantities of apples, bricks, haircuts, cheese, shoes, train journeys, sewing machines, glassware, cash registers or weedkiller that people buy does not give you a very useful statistic. The demand for apples may well affect the price of apples, but it is unlikely to do much to the price of sewing machines. Real, specific things may affect one another, but the mainstream economists' averages and aggregates are merely the statistical results of that process, not the things that create it.

Remember also, says Mises, that the way we react to things like prices is itself unpredictable. We are only human, after all. Specific price changes do influence individuals to rethink their spending priorities; but then different individuals – or even the same individuals at different times – may react quite differently. A rise in the price of sugar might cause some people to panic-buy in case the shops run out, for example, while others might see it as a good opportunity to cut down on sugar and change to a healthier diet.

So there can be no mechanical link between the mainstream economists' broad measures. Everything depends on the diverse and unpredictable choices of individuals, with their varied and changing priorities. This very individual, personal, *subjective* basis of economic life makes life hard for macroeconomists, whose search for constant relationships between statistical aggregates is necessarily misguided. And it makes life quite impossible for econometricians, who attempt to put numbers on these phantom relationships.

Mises was not the originator of this approach. It had been worked out by Carl Menger in his 1871 *Principles of Economics*, and was already the defining characteristic of the Austrian School, which Menger founded. The key contribution that Mises made, however, was to apply this thinking rigorously and systematically across the whole range of economic problems. In the process, he solved many questions that were thought previously insoluble, and exposed the fundamental errors of mainstream economics.

The nature and workings of money

An example of this is how Mises revealed the true nature and role of something so basic to economic life as money itself. Mainstream economists regarded money as merely a medium of exchange. It was not an 'economic good' that was 'demanded' or 'consumed' for its own sake (except, perhaps, by pathological misers). It seemed therefore to be more like a standard *measure* of worth, rather than something whose worth in any way depended on the valuation of individuals.

But Mises pointed out that the same market forces that determine the price of any other economic good also determine the 'price' of money. For example, the amount of money that people *demand* – how much of it they want to keep handy in their wallets, tills and bank accounts – depends on how useful they think it will be to them in making future exchanges. But like other economic goods, money is scarce: so the more they value it for its usefulness in exchange, and the more of it that people therefore demand, the higher rises its price – or what we normally call its *purchasing power*.

This radical piece of analysis was an astonishing achievement, especially since Mises had barely turned 30 when he wrote about it. He had shown that money was not something aloof and impersonal, but a reflection of human values; he had brought money within the scope of market analysis.

The business cycle

Such insights helped Mises explain something else that had long puzzled economists: the *business cycle* – the rhythmic ups and downs in business activity, prices and incomes that are seen over the years. He showed that the ultimate source of these cycles was a surge in bank credit – invariably encouraged by central banks and their political masters.

Since at least the eighteenth century, economists had known that when the quantity of money in circulation rises for some reason, people feel richer and spend more; but this extra spending merely drives up prices, leaving nobody better off. Such is the story of inflation. But Mises, alongside his colleague Friedrich Hayek, saw that it was worse than that. The spending boom makes entrepreneurs believe there is a real increase in demand for their products. Meanwhile, the surge in credit makes loans cheaper. So entrepreneurs borrow more to invest more and produce more.

But this is mistaken over-investment – *malinvestment* – based on false price signals. Before long, the public's spending spree is curbed by the rising prices. And at low interest rates, people will grow unwilling to save enough to finance businesses' new investment plans. Entrepreneurs then find themselves squeezed between falling demand and rising borrowing costs. Their new projects will have to be written off, and real resources are wasted. The false boom has led to a painful bust. According to Mises, only strict limits on the creation of money – such as a gold standard – will prevent such cycles and the damage they cause. Earlier economists had already thought about business cycles before Mises. But once again, Mises made a breakthrough by integrating various earlier ideas – on credit, on the structure of production and on interest rates – into a unified theory of economic booms and slumps. It was another dazzling achievement.

Capital, interest and time

Mises also gave us a better understanding of the nature of capital and interest. *Interest*, he maintained, is not a dead fact of nature – some automatic 'return' on saving. Rather, it arises from how the individuals involved value the future – specifically, whether they think it worth giving up consumption today in order to make the fishing nets, the ploughshares and the machinery that will make production more plentiful tomorrow. And this trade-off between consumption today and greater consumption tomorrow reveals the crucial importance of *time* in all economic calculations – something largely overlooked, or misunderstood, in the mainstream textbooks.

But, in trying to simplify things for students, the textbooks commit yet other fatal errors. One of these is to treat *capital* as homogeneous. Mises (building on the work of his Austrian School predecessor, Eugen von Böhm-Bawerk) argued that *capital* exists only in specific *capital goods*, each of which is different from the next. A steam hammer, for instance, is far different from an anvil and a mallet in terms of cost, function, flexibility of use and ease of relocation. So the exact *assortment* of capital goods that we possess can have a crucial bearing on the progress of our economy. By lumping different capital goods together as simply 'capital', macroeconomists overlook the possibility that people are investing in the *wrong sorts* of capital goods – *malinvestment* that, as Mises showed in his work on business cycles, must eventually lead to real losses.

The impossibility of socialist calculation

A fifth key contribution by Mises was his demolition of socialism, on the grounds that economic calculation simply becomes impossible when markets cease to exist. Where the means of production are owned by the state, and are thus never bought or sold, there is no way to price them. So we cannot know which of several possible production processes is the cheapest and therefore have no rational way to choose between them. Inevitably, over-expensive production processes will be chosen and resources will be wasted. The market economy, by contrast, puts a competitive pressure on producers to choose the most cost-effective processes – thus reducing waste and preserving vital resources intact for other purposes.

This was a particularly telling point during the debates on socialism that raged in Europe throughout the early twentieth century. In response to it, socialist theoreticians proposed 'market socialism', in which resources would be allocated 'as if' markets existed; or else they maintained that the issue of deciding between different production possibilities was merely a mathematical problem of solving large numbers of simultaneous equations.

But Mises retorted that market socialism could work only when there were *real* market prices for it to copy; so it could never spread too far, or there would be no real prices left to go on. As for the idea of mathematical planning, it ignored the fact that circumstances inevitably change while the plan is in progress: so the mathematician never has any 'simultaneous' data to digest – not that it is feasible to collect and digest so much data in the first place. Socialism, in other words, is simply not logically robust.

Teaching and influence

Mises had a wide and lasting influence that persists to this day. His most illustrious student, Friedrich Hayek, went on to win the Nobel Prize for work that they had both done on business cycles. Another admirer, Lionel (later Lord) Robbins, went on to be an adviser to the British government; another, Jacques Rueff, became economic adviser to General de Gaulle in France, and a third, Luigi Einaudi, became president of Italy.

In fact, Mises influenced an entire generation of free market economists and liberal social thinkers, including Fritz Machlup (who pioneered the economics of the information society), Gott-fried Haberler (who wrote influential works on international trade, opportunity costs, exchange rates and productive efficiency), Israel Kirzner (famed for his work on entrepreneurship), Murray Rothbard (author of the libertarian classic *Man, Economy, and State*), and many more. There are institutes named after him in both America and Europe. His books are used in colleges and universities across the world. And his iconoclastic ideas continue to spread.

2 LIFE, CAREER AND WRITINGS

Career in Europe and America

Ludwig von Mises was born in 1881, in Lemberg, Galicia (now Lviv in Ukraine), where his father was working on financing and constructing railroads.[1] But he grew up mainly in Vienna, entering the university in 1900, and graduating with a doctorate in law and economics in 1906. Like most students, he at first believed in the need for government intervention in the economy; but his discovery of Carl Menger's *Principles of Economics* converted him to the importance of free markets, and the conviction that individual choices were the only sound basis of economic enquiry.

Official economic posts

After graduating, Mises worked for the Austrian Chamber of Commerce, a semi-official body that advised the government on economic policy issues. He soon became its most prominent analyst – a status consolidated by the publication, in 1912, of his monumental book *The Theory of Money and Credit*.

---

1   For a more detailed biography, see Ludwig von Mises, *Notes and Recollections*, Liberation Press, South Holland, IL, 1978. See also Eamonn Butler, *Ludwig von Mises: Fountainhead of the Modern Microeconomics Revolution*, Gower, Brookfield, VT, and Aldershot, 1988.

Mises wanted to be an academic teacher, but never rose in that profession – barred, he believed, because of his unfashionable liberal, free market views. In 1913 he did begin teaching at the University of Vienna, but only as *Privatdozent*, having to rely on fees rather than a university salary.

After military service in World War I, Mises became director of the Reparations Commission, administering aspects of the peace settlement that broke up the Austro-Hungarian Empire. Here, he met and employed the young economist Friedrich Hayek; and he was able to resume as *Privatdozent* at the university, running a private seminar that brought together many fine liberal scholars.

Academic research

In 1922 Mises published another monumental book, *Socialism*. But his interest in money and credit persisted, and in 1927 he founded the Austrian Institute for Business Cycle Research, in which Hayek joined him. In the same year, he published *Liberalism*, in which he recast and restated the fundamental principles of a free society.

His work on business cycles did nothing to cheer Mises about the state of the Austrian economy. This was the period of the great hyperinflation in Germany; and Austria was not immune, with the currency falling so far that it took 14,400 paper crowns to be worth one gold crown. Mises correctly predicted that the inevitable result of the 1920s excesses would be a widespread collapse of the financial and banking system.

When invited to become Professor of International Economic Relations at the Graduate Institute of International Studies in Geneva, Mises accepted eagerly – though he maintained a part-time role with the Austrian Chamber of Commerce until Hitler annexed Austria in 1938. But his Jewish ancestry and fierce anti-totalitarianism left him an exile from Austria and an embarrassment to the Swiss government: in 1940, he and his wife Margit fled to the United States, where he became a citizen in 1946.[2]

Writing and teaching in America

Although his academic reputation preceded him, Mises was already in his sixties when he arrived in New York, and he struggled to find an academic post. Perhaps his relatively poor English and his prickly personality did not help. Between 1945 and 1969, however, he taught at New York University, though only as an unpaid visiting professor. Nevertheless, these years were very active. Mises attracted gifted students and teachers to his seminars, as he had done in Vienna. He produced books such as *Bureaucracy*, *Omnipotent Government*, *The Anti-Capitalist Mentality* and *Theory and History*, which exposed the deficiencies in non-liberal thinking and contained important new insights on the method of economic science. Then in 1949 his massive book *Human Action* integrated economics and individualism into an impressive whole. It is still regarded as his greatest work.

In his later years, Mises was recognised with honorary degrees and other accolades. He died in October 1973, the undisputed doyen of the Austrian School of economics. Exactly a year later, the news broke that his follower and friend Friedrich Hayek would receive the Nobel Prize for the business cycle theory that they had jointly pioneered.

---

2   His brother Richard, a prominent applied mathematician, had already emigrated to the United States a year earlier.

Writings on economics, political science and method

Throughout his adult life, Mises was uncompromising in his adherence to anti-statist beliefs. Even at the first meeting of the Mont Pèlerin Society – a group of liberal social thinkers founded by Hayek in 1947 – Mises stormed out during a discussion on progressive income taxes, exclaiming: 'You're all a bunch of socialists!' When his disciple Fritz Machlup once questioned the wisdom of a gold standard, Mises broke off relations with him for three years.

Perhaps, from his inter-war experiences in Europe, Mises knew the dangers of compromising with socialism. But socialist ideas were fashionable and his uncompromising views held back his academic career. Even his most densely theoretical works are often peppered with blistering polemics against the intellectual drift towards statism – something that academic readers can find unsettling.

Nor did it help that Mises wrote in German when the attention of economists was centred on English-language writers such as Fisher, Marshall and Keynes. Being outside that body of conventional wisdom, his works were slow to be translated; and some of those translations do scant justice to the precision of his original language. Even when he did write in English after moving to America, he lacked fluency: his meaning can be obscure and is often misrepresented by his choice of words. He sometimes darts, in the space of just a few pages, from the densest academic reasoning to the most cutting invective against ideas that he finds wanting. His caustic tirades in particular can put off modern readers. Yet even so, he is worth sticking with, since his work remains innovative, powerful and still relevant today.

Works on economic theory

His 1912 *Theory of Money and Credit* was a brilliant achievement. Large in scope and meticulous in detail, it brought microeconomic analysis to bear on the theory of money, credit and inflation. It was influential in continental Europe, though in Britain and America it was eclipsed by Irving Fisher's macroeconomic approach of a year earlier. But his work on money and credit, and in particular his explanation of business cycles as the inevitable result of credit-fuelled malinvestment, remains one of the most important contributions that Mises made to economic science.

Human Action is another great achievement, a bold restatement of economics as merely one part of a more general *science of human action*, which Mises calls *praxeology*. The principles of economics, it explained, can be deduced from a few self-evident axioms about human purposes and choices. It underlined the importance of how *individuals* react to events, and the crucial role of time, uncertainty and speculation in those decisions – all things largely ignored by mainstream macroeconomics. From this foundation, *Human Action* gives us a fresh understanding of the true nature of money, monopoly, competition, inflation, the role of government and much else.

Systems of social organisation

Mises believed that economics, rightly understood, could provide important guidance on what sorts of economic or social organisation were practicable or impracticable. His 1919 book *Nation, State, and Economy* is a fine example. It argues that nations, keen to preserve their culture, commonly resist immigration by other groups and raise protectionist barriers against them. The net effect is to trap other nations in poor and overpopulated areas, promoting resentment and prompting them to simply grasp the territory they 'need'. But it is the power of governments to raise barriers which sparks these conflicts; only the demise of that state power will end them.

Socialism, then, is a recipe for conflict. Socialist economies have to insulate themselves, or migration would upset their careful plans. And socialist states are inherently imperialist: market economies always outshine them; so to preserve the myth of their superiority, they have to try to socialise all other states.

Mises developed these views in another great book, *Socialism*, in 1922. It makes many biting points, but its most devastating theme was that rational economic calculation was impossible under socialism: without prices, there is no way of knowing whether production goods are being used cost-effectively.

His 1929 *A Critique of Interventionism* showed that watered-down socialism is no better. Any intervention in markets, it explains, produces unexpected and undesirable side effects. Keeping down the price of milk, for example, raises the demand for milk but makes it less profitable for producers to supply it. Inevitably, shortages arise: so governments intervene again to correct things – and so on, until, before long, piecemeal intervention turns into full socialism. Always a great polemicist, Mises took up the same theme in other books, such as *Planning for Freedom* and *Economic Policy*.

In the short, readable 1944 monograph *Bureaucracy*, Mises showed how civil servants could never be entrepreneurs. Businesses, he says, face one simple test – profitability; but government bodies face the impossible problem of juggling numerous, competing political demands. Also in 1944, his book *Omnipotent*

Government restated how interventionism lowers productivity and leads to demands to acquire more profitable territory, fuelling the nationalism and imperialism that lead to war.

Liberalism, published in 1927, is an elegant statement of the only alternative. Economic prosperity, it says, depends on specialisation and trade. But these exist only where the means of production are privately owned and people are free to exchange. That requires peace and liberty, which experience tells us require equal civil and political rights. Liberals would limit the state's role to enforcing these rights and preserving peace: it is all too easy for governments to erode private property if they have the power to do so. Liberalism, however, is a force for peace, Mises says: where people depend on trade with others, they are less likely to go to war with them.

Methodological works

Mises wrote three technical books on economic theory and method. It was in the 1933 *Epistemological Problems of Economics* that he outlined the point that economics is not an experimental science like physics, but a deductive system more like mathematics, in which every theorem can be *deduced* from the simple axiom that individuals act purposively. From this foundation, the ideas of preferences, costs, time, interest and much else come naturally. Only *observation* can tell us exactly *what* people choose; but this method of *deduction* tells us *how* they choose – and that is what economics is actually about.

The Ultimate Foundations of Economic Science, published in 1962, again showed why the experimental methods of the natural sciences are unsuited to economics. We act, says Mises, because we *value* certain things, and from that obvious point we can derive the ideas of ends, means, success, failure, profit and loss. The economist needs nothing else. The method of observation and experiment is inappropriate in economics because there are no measurable constants and no way of forecasting the actions of individuals whose values and purposes we cannot know. The belief that human society is predictable is precisely what produces the statist conceit that it is also controllable.

The 1957 *Theory and History* applied this critique to other disciplines. It is partly a criticism of Marxian theory and method, and partly a defence of liberalism. It argues that the unpredictability of human choices makes nonsense of the idea that socialism, or any other historical development, is 'inevitable'. But it also makes the important point that all economic data are about events that have already happened. As we struggle to refine theories that tell us how the world works, we need to remember that the data we base them on are all history. They may inform our ideas, but they cannot tell us for sure what will happen tomorrow, because by tomorrow the world will be different.

The legacy of Mises today

Mises was pessimistic about the impact of his contribution on economic and political theory. He hoped his writings would have a more immediate effect; but during his lifetime, socialism and interventionism remained fashionable.

Since his death, however, the shortcomings of real-world socialist societies have been vividly exposed. At the same time, trade liberalisation has raised living standards in the world's poorest countries and made allies out of formerly imperialist, warring nations. The idea that trade cycles are caused by inept monetary and credit policy is now widely accepted. And the transition from mass production to a more customised service economy has underlined the crucial importance of individuals over impersonal forces.

All in all, the work of Ludwig von Mises has far more traction today than he once feared.

3 THE SCIENCE OF ECONOMICS

Economists want their discipline to be scientific. Like the natural scientists, they want to show linkages between things, and to make predictions about how they will behave in the future. Mises took the view that economics is indeed scientific, but in a way quite unlike that of the physical sciences. And while it can make important predictions, these again are of quite a different kind and accuracy.[1]

The importance of values

The difference is that all economic phenomena depend on the values, choices and actions of the *individuals* involved. Mainstream economists talk as if one economic variable – *the price level*, say – has a direct effect on another – such as *aggregate demand*. In fact, there is no such thing as a price 'level', but millions of specific prices, each fluctuating against one another. Different prices will affect the decisions of different individuals in different ways, depending on their specific personal needs and outlook, and how they value the options on offer at that particular time and place.

There is nothing mechanical about this: so economics can

---

1   See *Epistemological Problems of Economics* for the full explanation of this approach.

never be about predictable statistical linkages between things. Economic concepts like prices, costs, money, unemployment, exchange rates, expenditures and savings have no importance except in terms of their *meaning* to the individuals concerned, and how those individuals act as a result. Economics is rooted in human *values*.

But values are not part of the *objective* world, like the mass or temperature or length that natural scientists deal with. Value is not something that exists in goods themselves which can be measured on some mathematical scale. Different people value things differently: some people might see a rising stock market price as a good reason to buy, for example, and others as a good opportunity to sell. Value is in the mind of the individual. It is something emotional, a matter of personal judgement. It depends not just on our physical environment, but on our current psychological and physiological state too.

And our values *change*, because our world changes and our needs change. New products spring up and new processes make alternative goods cheaper, causing people to reorder their priorities. The results are unpredictable: the mass production of a fashion item, for example, might make it affordably attractive to the poor, but no longer appealing to the fashion-conscious rich.

The fact that human values are personal, different and changing poses problems for the economist. Familiar macroeconomic aggregates such as 'demand' or 'investment' must then be seen as merely statistical summaries of individuals' actions in the marketplace – actions that are diverse, personal and far from uniform. These statistics have no independent life. They cannot be explained without reference to the personal values of the individuals who are moved by, and who in turn shape, specific events.[2]

Economists therefore waste their time trying to search out statistical linkages between macroeconomic aggregates, says Mises. For example, even though it may be obvious that prices affect demand, it is equally plain that the relationship is never precise. The exact outcome rests on the *meaning* of the particular events to the individuals who are there at the time and on what they do as a result. The search for economic 'laws' (or, even worse, 'constants') is misguided.

The science of human action

Although economics is rooted in human values, it is not a branch of psychology. It is not about *why* people choose particular things – why they drink alcohol, say – only the *results* of those choices in the marketplace – how much alcohol they demand, at what prices. Economics has to take individuals' values and purposes as 'givens'. It focuses solely on their actions. It is, says Mises, part of the more general science of human action, *praxeology*. And to describe this scientific study of human economic actions – how prices emerge from the buzz of human exchange activity – he uses the term *catallactics*. The overall outcome of such exchanges he calls a *catallaxy* – fearing that the term *the economy* makes it all sound far too mechanical, deliberate and planned.

But as a science, catallactics is quite different from the natural sciences, which discover things and make useful predictions through a programme of observation and testing. For one thing,

---

2   This approach is known as *methodological individualism*.

the economist has no apparatus with which to observe other people's values. And secondly, economic outcomes can never be tested because the exact circumstances can never be replicated: the individuals, their choices, their values and their motives are constantly changing.

Nevertheless, economics *is* a science that can discover things and even make predictions, claims Mises – not on the basis of observation and testing, but through a process of *deduction*. Just as geometry or mathematics can be derived from a few simple and obvious axioms about line and number, so the science of human action can be deduced from the very concept of action and choice itself.

Interpreting values from actions

We cannot see into the minds of individuals and discover what causes them to act in a particular way, says Mises; but this does not stop us treating their actual *choices* scientifically. We can still build up theories of demand and price (say), however inaccessible and personal their ultimate origin happens to be.

Indeed, we can build up a picture of human values from the practical choices that people actually make. A person's actual choices in the marketplace, explains Mises, show what things the person in fact prefers, and so reveal something about their scale of values – what he calls *demonstrated preference*. We cannot see people's values, but we can *infer* them from what each person actually chooses.

We know from our own minds that when we choose one thing over another, it is because we *prefer* it over the other. And obviously, what we choose to have is more important to us than what we leave behind or give up to get it. Likewise, when we see other people make a choice, we presume that their action too is motivated by their own values and preferences. When we see them make a *series* of choices, selecting some things and leaving others, we conclude that, like ourselves, each individual possesses an extended *scale of values*.

We can now begin to glimpse what Mises means when he says that the principles of economics can be deduced from the concept of action itself. When people act and make choices, it implies that they have a set of values and that they consider some things more important than others. Without needing to know exactly what any individual actually chooses, the *logic* of choice gives us the fundamental ideas of economics – ideas like utility, cost and exchange.

The example of utility analysis

What economists call *marginal utility analysis* is a good example of this approach at work. For a century, economists struggled with the problem that something like water, so essential to life, was cheap, while diamonds, so inessential, were expensive. Why should diamonds be valued so much more than water?

The founder of the Austrian School of economics, Carl Menger, provided the answer. Individuals are not choosing between 'water' and 'diamonds' in the abstract: they do not face the choice of having all the water in the world, or all the world's diamonds. The only choice is whether they would like some small volume of water, or a new diamond. And the fact is that most people already have enough water for their satisfaction, so they do not really value an extra cupful: that is why water is cheap.

But people never believe they have too many diamonds, and are willing to pay handsomely for an extra one: that is why diamonds are expensive.

A person in the desert, of course, might value a cup of water very highly indeed, and could be willing to sacrifice a fortune in diamonds for it. So there is no fixed 'quantity of value' that exists in water and in diamonds; what people choose depends entirely on the *actual quantities* they are presented with and on their *personal circumstances* and state of mind at that moment.

This all means that values and choices cannot be measured and predicted in neat mathematical equations. Someone with a headache might welcome a couple of aspirins, but would not think that a hundred aspirins were fifty times better. A person who needs ten logs to complete a shelter might exchange a raincoat for ten, twenty or thirty logs: but not for nine, which would not keep out the rain. There is no arithmetic by which, from people's valuation of a certain quantity of things, we can scale up or down to know how they will value a different quantity.

Faulty thinking in mainstream economics

When people are presented with an exchange, in which they have to give up some of what they have in return for something else they want, how do they make the choice? The answer, said the Austrian School economists, is that they give up whatever is bringing them least benefit. They do not have to consider the value of everything they own: only the value of the bit of it that is least useful to them. They decide what to give up on the basis of *marginal utility*, as economists call it. And similarly, they decide what they will accept in exchange in exactly the same manner.

They will accept something that is more useful to them than what they give up only if its *marginal utility* to them is greater.

Much of this analysis has found its way into mainstream economics, though it is often misunderstood. Many people treat *utility* as a quality that exists in goods, rather than as each individual's emotional reaction to a good. At its worst, says Mises, this is found in textbooks where 'blocks' of 'utility' are added up to show a graph of 'total utility'. But human emotions, human values, cannot be measured and added up like this – as the aspirin example shows.

The familiar textbook 'indifference curves' are equally flawed. These smooth graphs purport to show how much of one thing an individual will give up for another. But we cannot extrapolate from the decisions that people have made when faced with real-world choices to say how they *would* react to some other set of choices. Human values are not so smooth and predictable – as in the logs example.

Faulty thinking like this stores up trouble for mainstream economists, believes Mises. On the basis of a few observations about actual choices in the past, they claim they can identify 'propensities' (say, to consume or to save) that are measurable and constant, allowing them to make predictions about future choices. But all these constructions are utterly unreal. Mises points out that a person's past preferences cannot tell us how they will react to some different, real choice in the future – much less a hypothetical one.

In part, that is because mainstream economics overlooks the true richness of human values. It focuses only on 'economic goods' – things that can be traded in the marketplace – and sees people as 'rational agents' choosing between them. In reality, explains

Mises, people's choices are far wider and more emotional than this. Individuals may choose personal honour over financial gain, for example. Mainstream economics misses this important half of the story. Thereby, it invalidates its own theories.

4 THE LOGIC OF HUMAN ACTION

The fact of conscious human *action* is intuitively obvious, says Mises; and action is simply our pursuit of a *preferred* situation over a less preferred one. From that intuitive notion of preferences, we can see straight away that people *act* to maximise their satisfaction and minimise their dissatisfaction. From this follow ideas like marginal utility and exchange: people will give up the things that give them least satisfaction in return for things that give them more. We do not need observation and experiment to know this: it all follows logically from the concept of action itself.[1] It does not matter what the particular values of the individual happen to be: *whatever* their preferences and needs are, the logic of action is that they will satisfy the most pressing ones first.

The same reasoning enables us to build up a picture of other economic concepts such as *ends and means* or *profit and loss*.[2]

An *end*, says Mises, is the result sought by an action; the *means* is what serves that goal. But, of course, resources are limited – this

---

1 Though his Austrian School follower, the Nobel economist F. A. Hayek, was 'reluctant to accept' that economic science could be derived wholly from self-evident truths, because that denied the possibility of the unexpected happening, and so devalued the importance of practical observation, 'although I agree with him that much of it consists merely in working out the logical implications of certain initial facts'. See 'Coping with ignorance', in E. Butler (ed.), *Knowledge, Evolution and Society*, Adam Smith Institute, 1983.

2 See *Human Action* for a comprehensive statement of the arguments summarised in this chapter.

is another truism that follows from the concept of action, since people would not bother to act at all if they had a full sufficiency of everything they desired. And because resources are limited, our *means* themselves are limited. So we have to make choices between them, and sacrifice some things to achieve others.

The value to us of what we give up is what we call the *cost*. Our valuation of the end we achieve as a result is called the *benefit*. And the difference between the cost and the benefit we call the *profit* (or, if things go badly, the *loss*).

But these economic concepts – cost, benefit, profit and loss – are all entirely *personal*. They are our emotional judgements about value. They are not *objective* – observable and measurable like the things that natural scientists deal with – but *subjective* – something that takes place in the mind of the person involved. These things can no more be subjected to mathematical analysis than can any other emotion, such as grief, envy or love.

The origins of exchange and prices

And this highly personal nature of value, cost, benefit, profit and loss is why we trade and exchange things. If value were an objective quality of things, something like their size or weight, we would never exchange anything. Nobody would exchange one good for another that was plainly worth less. But we *do* exchange things; and we do so precisely *because* we value things differently. Children swap toys they are bored with for others they want. The baker sells bread in order to buy meat from the butcher. No new toys, nor bread or meat, are created by the exchange – but everyone considers themselves better off because of it. Indeed, they would not bother to trade things if they did not.

Of course, we can never know or measure how much psychological *profit* each party derives from such transactions. But we can at least see and measure the amount of one thing that they are prepared to give up to get another – the amount of money, for example, that the baker demands in exchange for a loaf of bread. And that rate of exchange is what we call the *price*. In a primitive barter economy, the price of a loaf might be so much meat, or so much of some other good. But in the modern economy, where we use money as a medium of exchange, price is expressed in dollars, pounds or the relevant local currency.

Nevertheless, we must remember that *prices*, though plainly observable, are not in fact a measure of the *value* of things. The *market price* for bread, or meat, or any other good, is simply the *rate of exchange* that emerges as a result of many individuals all trading these things in the marketplace. And that trade happens only because people value these things *differently*. Each exchange involves only one *price*, but two different and conflicting *valuations*.

The false foundations of textbook economics

This simple reasoning, says Mises, shows the absurdity of mainstream economic models. Of course, the textbook case of 'perfect competition' is intended merely as a simplification of the real world. But a model in which all buyers and sellers are identical, and no buyer or seller has any impact on the price of the goods traded, is not a simplification of the real world, but a complete renunciation of it. Markets work only *because* people are *not* identical, and prices emerge only *because* people exchange on the basis of *different* valuations.

Nor are prices merely a 'given', as the models suggest. There can be nothing given, or even consistent, about prices because they are the result of countless transactions between diverse and changing human beings, each facing various and changing choices. The textbook notion of the 'equilibrium price' at which supply and demand balances is plainly nonsense. And attempts to build a model of 'general equilibrium' at which all markets are in balance are an even bigger folly. These models *assume away* everything that makes markets work.

Mises was not the first person to say all this: earlier Austrian School economists developed the idea that individual value judgements were at the heart of every economic event and pioneered the analysis of marginal utility and the critique of mainstream theories. The powerful contribution that Mises made, however, was to collate and hone these early, various, often disjointed thoughts into a comprehensive approach to economics as a deductive, rather than experimental, science – an approach of which he was, beyond dispute, the most robust defender.

5 THE DYNAMIC ECONOMY

For Mises, the textbook models of an economy in perfect balance, with prices determined by impersonal forces, rob economics of its life and soul. The whole basis of economics is human *action*, and human action means *change* – the replacement of one state by another.[1]

Change is inherent in economics

We live in a world of change. Natural events and conditions change: there are good and bad harvests, new resources are discovered and old ones become exhausted or dilapidated, or are accidentally destroyed by fire or flood. Human conditions also change: populations grow and shift, and younger members replace the older ones, bringing fresh ideas with them. Production methods change too, with new processes being invented and old ones fading into disuse.

Thanks in part to Mises and his Austrian School colleagues, modern economists now recognise the importance of change rather better. But the textbooks are still full of graphs, models and equations that give the misleading impression that the economy is somehow fixed and static. An example is 'equilibrium theory'

---

1   See *Human Action* for the systematic presentation of this argument.

– the idea that, at some price level, markets reach a state of balance when the quantity of a product that sellers wish to supply exactly equals the quantity that buyers want to buy. And since markets are interconnected – the market for grain affects the market for bread, for example – the textbooks imagine the possibility of a world of 'general equilibrium' in which every market comes to rest in the same perfect balance.

But markets are never at rest. Just look at the fluctuating prices on the stock exchange, says Mises. They are more like a table-tennis ball on the top of a jet of water, jerking around as gravity pulls it one way and the jet pushes it another. A snapshot photo might give the impression that the ball is in perfect stasis, but it is not. Similarly, a snapshot of the economy – the classic textbook graph in which supply and demand curves cross over at some 'equilibrium price', for example – gives an equally false impression of stability. The proper role of the economist is not to present a snapshot, insists Mises, but to understand the changing *forces* that keep markets in motion, like the changing forces that keep the table-tennis ball bobbing around in the air.

Even where the textbooks do talk about change, they are utterly misleading. The classic graph, for example, suggests that if supply or demand changes, the market will instantly snap back to some new point of balance, at a new equilibrium price, with new quantities being traded. But markets simply do not work like this. Market movements are neither instantaneous nor smooth. In reality, it takes time for people to notice shortages or surpluses, and to act on them; their information may be inaccurate; and it takes time to manufacture new supplies and bring them to market. In short, there is no reason to suppose that anything close to equilibrium will ever prevail.

The real nature of markets

So markets can never be anything like the 'perfect' models of the textbooks. Buyers and sellers are all different – and as human individuals, they have many motives besides simply maximising their financial returns. The goods they exchange have a range of different qualities, and indeed are unique in terms of the time and place in which they are traded. Information about what quantities are being traded, and at what price, does not spread out evenly or instantly. Technology and preferences change. And, crucially, everything takes time.

These are no mere 'imperfections' that can be assumed or legislated away: they are the very reality of markets and should be our starting point for analysing them. This reality will certainly never deliver the blissful imaginary state of general equilibrium. But markets work only *because* there are differences that people can exploit, and unsatisfied needs that they can help satisfy. If the world were always in perfect balance, there would be no motivation for anyone to do anything at all, and economic life would cease to exist.

The aim of policy, therefore, should not be to try to make markets *perfect*, but to allow them to work efficiently within their real nature. And as Mises reminds us, we should never assume that they could ever work as smoothly as the gentle curves of the textbook models suggest. Markets adjust through the discrete choices of individuals, each with their own particular values, and each having to work around the unfolding choices of others. That will never be a smooth and predictable process, but a series of jerky and unpredictable steps.

Why mathematics is inappropriate

This is why equilibrium theorists simply compound their errors when they try to apply mathematics to what they suppose are smooth adjustments. They end up putting numbers on things that do not actually exist. The trappings of their mathematics might make it look as if they have discovered the kind of functional relationships that natural scientists deal with; but they are not describing the real world, merely something from their own imagination.

And no amount of statistics, Mises believes, can overcome the essential point that different people have different values, and that the response of one set of individuals to market events today may not be the same as others to events tomorrow. Values cannot be subjected to mathematical analysis, and the use of statistics simply masks everything that is important in economic life. True, it might be possible to make broad predictions about economic events – that an expansion of credit will create a boom followed by a bust, for example – but we can never predict exactly how pronounced or how lengthy that cycle will be.

The market process

To Mises, then, the proper study of economics is a study of the forces that keep markets in perpetual motion – how the various actions of diverse individuals, each pursuing their own objectives in the market, mesh together to produce the result they do. In other words, economics should study the market *process* by which people adjust their actions to events, including the actions of others.

This idea of the market as a process of continuous change is at odds with the textbook notion of stable, permanent equilibrium. There may well be *forces* that tend to keep things in balance, like the forces of gravity and water pressure that keep the table-tennis ball in the air: where there are shortages, for example, prices may well rise, inducing buyers to cut back their demand and sellers to supply more until the gap is filled. But the existence of these forces does not mean that a perfect, durable balance will ever be achieved. The world changes, people change, and products and production processes change. Markets never actually come to rest.

The critical importance of time

The textbooks hardly mention it, but *time* is a crucial part of the market process. Mises – following the earlier Austrian economist Eugen von Böhm-Bawerk – points out that all action takes time. While action is in progress, other events can change and perhaps thwart it. During the time it takes for people to spot and adjust to market changes, things might change yet again. A new factory might take months or years to build, for example; but in the meantime, consumer tastes may turn against its product, or some revolutionary new production process could make the factory redundant.

The textbook notion of smooth and instant adjustment towards equilibrium, concludes Mises, blinds us to the pivotal importance of time in the market process. It also blinds us to the *uncertainty* that prevails in economic life. In the textbook world, everything is known and certain, and markets gravitate to a predictable point of balance. In reality, the outcome of our actions is far from certain. Some plans will succeed, while unexpected events will cause others to fail. We do not know for sure where things will take us. Every move we make is therefore a *specula-tion* – an action based on a guess about the future, which may or may not turn out to be correct. It is this which makes the textbook models so wrong; and which makes the role of speculation and entrepreneurship such a crucial element of the economics of the real world.

6 ENTREPRENEURSHIP

In the textbook world of 'perfect competition', *profit* is merely the residue that is left to suppliers after they have paid their capital, labour and distribution costs. Competition will beat it down to the lowest level necessary to tempt suppliers to remain in the market – a 'normal return' that will be the same for everyone. But, says Mises, there can be little spur to innovation when everyone receives the same margin, regardless of their skill, drive or luck. In the real world, profit is much more than this. It is a crucial motivator of human action. To understand economics, we need to understand the true nature and role of entrepreneurship and profit.[1]

Entrepreneurship and profit

The production of any commodity involves much more than just employing capital in any way you choose and enjoying the 'normal return' that it generates. In reality, production involves complex choices. Complementary factors of production such as land, labour and equipment have to be brought together. Inevitably, it all takes some time. To make a financial gain, the promoter of the project – the *entrepreneur* – must be able to sell the final product

---

1   See *Human Action* for the arguments concerning entrepreneurship and profit.

at a price higher than the price of the various inputs. But since production takes time, and things can change during the interval, this outcome is by no means certain: the cost of inputs may rise along the way, other competitors may enter the market and bid for customers, new and better products or processes might be developed, fashions might change, or customers might not in fact prove willing to pay what the producer anticipated.

All production, therefore, is a *speculation*. It is an attempt to guess the future state of the market. It involves taking a *risk*, and there is no guarantee of a successful outcome. Success will hinge on a mixture of knowledge, skill and luck. Profit is not simply a return on the amount of capital employed in any random venture. It is absurd to speak of a 'rate of profit' on something so uncertain. Profit is far more elusive than that.

What Mises calls *entrepreneurship* or *speculation* is not confined to a few sharp-suited wheeler-dealer capitalists of the popular imagination. Because of the inevitable uncertainties involved, *all action*, he says, is a speculation, and *all people* are to some degree entrepreneurs – seeking to use their resources and skills to produce future profit. That is as true of workers who take training courses in the hope of improving their job prospects as of the business executives who build factories or the stockbrokers who trade securities.[2]

There is no way of knowing for sure whether the ventures on which we choose to embark will pay off. We just have to take a guess at how the future will turn out. Profit provides a *motivation* to make our guess as accurate as possible – using whatever skill, judgement, experience, understanding and inside knowledge we

---

2   The importance of entrepreneurship is developed in greater depth in the work of Israel M. Kirzner, an Austrian School follower of Mises.

have. So too does the possibility of loss if we guess wrongly. Profit is not a dead fact: profit has a life and a *meaning* to purposive human beings.

Profit is a reward from satisfied customers

Profit, says Mises, is not just personal gain. It is not a measure of the happiness that we get from some successful action. Rather, profit encapsulates *other people's* valuation of what our initiative has contributed to *their* lives and welfare. It arises solely through the willing support of satisfied customers. Profit is a social phenomenon that reflects the values of all concerned.

Again, the textbook 'normal return' models seem to suggest that one entrepreneur can make a large ('supernormal') profit only if another makes a large loss. From this comes the idea that profit is 'exploitation' – something stolen from other people. But, says Mises, the rewards of any successful business are inevitably shared with the workers and those who provide the many inputs that it requires. And since profit comes only because consumers value the product, then the greater the profits being won, the greater is the increase in general prosperity.

The pricing process

The success of any entrepreneurial venture rests on making good guesses about future prices. But given that things change all the time, this is not easy. The textbooks may suggest that markets instantly snap back to a known 'equilibrium price' following any disturbance: but in fact, says Mises, price adjustment is more like an avalanche. Any change – the discovery of new mineral resources, say – is first noticed by only a few individuals who are near to it. Of those, only some will fully recognise its importance, correctly anticipate its effects, and swiftly take the right actions to profit by it; but their success will inspire others to follow. Those in turn will inspire others, and so on, making the market adjustment more and more widespread.

The spreading adjustment itself may set off other avalanches – bidding up the price of the mining equipment that is needed to take advantage of the new mineral discoveries, for example. Meanwhile, quite separate price avalanches caused by unrelated changes elsewhere may also impinge on the first. In other words, price adjustment is neither instant nor mechanical. It is a very complex process – a *social* process, says Mises. And the whole thing depends on precisely what the textbooks ignore – individual values and time and place.

The prices of production goods

Like the market prices of the goods we actually consume (what economists call *consumption goods*), the prices of production goods (the materials and capital equipment we use to make them) also derive from the *differences* in people's values. But the process is less direct, says Mises. Production goods, he explains, are not wanted for themselves, but only for the consumption goods they create. They are appraised, accordingly, on the anticipated price of those consumption goods.

Once again, the market process rewards those who make the most accurate guesses. An entrepreneur who has too pessimistic a view about future product prices will be priced out of the competition for productive resources, and will lose land, equipment and workers to others who take a more optimistic view. Meanwhile, an over-optimistic entrepreneur, willing to pay more for those assets, will suffer losses when the final product is marketed. Only those who make accurate guesses about the future prices of consumption goods will succeed.

This process therefore keeps the prices of production goods in step with the prices of consumption goods. It systematically prompts people to steer productive resources towards the uses where consumer demand is strongest. It constantly urges them to seek out the best and cheapest ways of satisfying those needs.

Like everything else in economics, then, it is the decisions of the *particular individuals* involved which drive things. The entrepreneurial function is largely overlooked in mainstream economics, yet it is critical to how markets work.

Entrepreneurs may be motivated by their own profit, but Mises is in no doubt that they are the *servants* of consumers. In a world of perpetual change, they have to stay constantly on the lookout for opportunities through which they can gain by serving others. The net effect is to increase the prosperity of the whole society. And a key factor in making this all happen efficiently is *competition*.

7 COMPETITION, COOPERATION AND THE CONSUMER

The textbook model of 'perfect competition' makes people imagine that the real world is somehow 'imperfect' – that differences between suppliers, natural obstacles to market entry and in particular any large profits enjoyed by entrepreneurs represent market 'failures' that must be corrected. But Mises insists that competition cannot even exist in a world where everybody and everything is the same. Competition is all about suppliers trying to outdo each other – and make a profit from so doing.[1]

The sovereignty of consumers

Competition sharpens the process by which entrepreneurial activity steers production to where it brings most satisfaction to consumers. The greater the competition, the more accurate producers have to be in anticipating the future demands of the public; and the more imaginative they have to be in serving them.

As in any walk of life, competition is a process of selection. But Mises points out that in markets, it is *consumers* who do the selecting. Consumers are always seeking out the best and cheapest products to satisfy their needs: it is *their* demand which ultimately decides the price of consumer goods – and therefore, indirectly, of

---

1   These themes are addressed in various books by Mises, such as *Human Action, Liberalism, Economic Policy* and *Planning for Freedom*.

producer goods. And they are hard bosses, willing to drop existing suppliers in a moment if better or cheaper ones come on to the scene.

The market, Mises concludes, is like a daily referendum on what should be produced. Every penny spent by consumers, in countless daily transactions, acts like a vote in a continual ballot, determining how much of each and every thing should be produced and drawing production to where it is most urgently required. As a way of allocating resources, this system is much more efficient than taking decisions through political elections, where people get the opportunity to vote only every few years and have to choose between packages of disparate policies.

Critics argue that it is not an equal election, since some people have more money 'votes' than others; but Mises sees things differently. First, every penny really *does* count: even the poorest have more leverage in the market than minorities have in political elections. Moreover, the cumulative impact of the modest 'votes' of millions of less well-off individuals can easily swamp those of a few rich ones; so consumer sovereignty remains a very powerful effect. And though a few well-off people might have more spending power, this is only because they have succeeded in previous 'ballots' and have satisfied their customers. Their market power, such as it is, comes ultimately from consumers and lasts only as long as consumers remain satisfied.

The process of competition

To Mises, then, competition is a continual *process* in which sellers try to surpass each other in order to deliver to consumers what they most want. It works *only because of* what the models see as 'imperfections' – because sellers offer their customers a *variety* of different products of different qualities, for example, and are continually striving to make their own offering slightly better or cheaper than those being offered by other people.

The fact that there are natural barriers to entry – we cannot all be opera singers, after all – does not make competition any less sharp. It may take only one or two competitors, producing better or cheaper products, to keep suppliers on their toes. But certainly, the keener the competition, the better it serves its social function of driving improvements in production and consumer satisfaction.

Again, critics say that competition is vicious or unjust. But market competition is not like a war, where the losers get killed: in the market, those who serve consumers less successfully simply get less reward. Firms do indeed go out of business from time to time, and people lose their money and their jobs; but the metaphor of firms being 'killed' by competition is not in the same league as the reality of defeated populations being machine-gunned by the victors. Nor are profits – even large profits – unjust, says Mises: on the contrary, they are in fact the just reward for serving consumers particularly well.

Cooperation through the division of labour

Far from being a war between all, the market process in fact encourages human cooperation on a huge scale. As Adam Smith first explained, it does this by encouraging *specialisation and exchange*.[2]

---

2   See Adam Smith, *The Wealth of Nations*, Book I, 1776.

Mises takes up the same theme. People are different, he says, with different abilities. They live in different places where there are different natural resources to hand. Breaking production down into discrete, specialist steps uses their various abilities and resources much more productively than if they all tried to be self-sufficient. And by then exchanging these specialist products, they can collaborate on the creation of projects and consumer goods that would be far beyond the abilities of any one of them.

In this system of specialisation and exchange, the productive resources are necessarily *owned* by particular individuals. But that does not mean that these owners are somehow opposed to the rest of society, as Marx claims. On the contrary, those who own the means of production can turn it to their personal benefit *only* by making their resources serve the consuming public.

Capitalism does not lead to monopoly

Another criticism made of market competition is that it actually promotes monopoly capitalism. Marx suggested that, as competition steadily whittled out the less successful enterprises, the remaining firms would get larger and larger, until there was just one monopoly producer left in each sector.

This is nonsense, says Mises: the reality is quite different. While it is easy to see the growth of large, successful firms, we invariably overlook the decline of the – equally large – firms that are replaced by up-and-coming ones. The market is not a process of inevitable concentration, but of constant jostling and change.

What worries people about monopoly is that dominant firms could charge any price they like. But even this is not so, says Mises. There will always be the threat of competition, perhaps from smaller, more innovative firms. And likewise there will always be substitutes that customers can turn to: the market dominance of America's railroad companies, for example, was broken by the rise of the airlines.

Socialism as the source of monopoly

In fact, says Mises, monopoly would be at its zenith under socialism, where all production is in state hands. The real source of monopoly, and a malign one, is not capitalism, but government.

Unlike commercial enterprises, which survive only if they continue to serve their consumers, governments can simply vote themselves monopolies – as they have done in the past for salt, telephones, broadcasting and much else. Or they create monopolies by restricting entry to certain professions, through *licensing*. Their justification may be public safety – so that people are not exposed to unqualified doctors or taxi drivers, for example. But all too often, Mises believes, the real motive is political. Licences can generate a healthy revenue for the authorities. And licensing will help those already in the market – who have more wealth and probably more political influence – to keep out potential competition.

Few cartels and monopolies would ever have come into being, he concludes, had it not been for government and the efforts of those with political power to stifle competition. Capitalism has no natural tendency to monopoly or monopoly prices; on the contrary, it has a powerful tendency towards diversity and differentiation, which bids quality up and prices down. The textbook models conceal it, but that is the whole point, and the enduring benefit, of the process of competition.

8 CAPITAL AND INTEREST

Like everything else in economics, says Mises, *capital* and *interest* spring out of the decisions of individuals – specifically, their different decisions about the value of *time*.[1]

The importance of time in human choices

Achieving almost any of our goals takes *time*. There may be many steps involved; and even then, what we achieve may require further effort to maintain it. In economic terms, time is needed to produce economic goods – what Mises calls the *period of production* – and they may last a limited time – the *period of provision*. So immediately that we embark on production, he says, we face choices: not just about the means we are going to use, but about our time preferences. Do we prefer to spend more time making a quality product that will serve us a long time? Or do we want to make something less durable but quicker to produce? There is no indisputably right answer to this: it depends entirely on the values of those involved.

How we *value* time is an essential element in every action we take. Everyone prefers satisfaction now to equal satisfaction later; though some people value immediate satisfaction highly, and

---

1   For the main discussion on this, see *Human Action* and *The Theory of Money and Credit*.

consume everything they earn, while others save, sacrificing satisfaction now for (they hope) greater satisfaction in the future.

Clearly, someone consuming $100-worth of goods today plainly values this immediate consumption more than the $104 or so that the money would become worth in a year's time if it were saved in a bank account. If time had no value to them, they would always prefer to have the $104 in a year's time. But our time is limited and it *does* have a value to us. And individual human beings' time preferences are the key to understanding the phenomenon of *interest*.

Mises gives an expressive example. You can catch fish by plucking them by hand from a stream. You might be able to catch many more fish with a net and a canoe – but these things take time to build. You may need to go hungry while you are working on this equipment, or build up stocks of fish to keep you going. But *postponing consumption* to create these *capital goods* is the route to a much more plentiful supply in the future: you might even start to catch new varieties of fish that you could never catch by hand. Yet it will be your personal choice whether those benefits later are worth the cost of going hungry right now.

The complexities of capital

Capital, concludes Mises, is something rather complex; and as always, human values, purposes and preferences are intimately bound up in it. The key thing that capital goods encapsulate is *time* – the sacrifice of consumption now for greater consumption later. Whether and how capital goods are used is not just a matter of having the right technology: it depends on the time preferences of those concerned. You might know how to make canoes and nets, but judge that the time and sacrifice involved are just not worth it.

Capital goods are intermediate steps on the way to consumption, which is the sole end of production. But that does not mean that the more a country spends on 'capital', the more productive it must be. Its productivity depends on the specific mix of capital goods that exist. For example, a shipyard, a steelworks and a coal mine might be utterly dependent on each other's products, while any one by itself might be quite useless.

In other words, it is not the *total spending* on capital goods which is important, but what and where they are, and how they are used – in other words, the *capital structure*. And this capital structure is critical in determining how an economy responds to change. Capital goods are all different: some, like a hammer, can be used for many purposes; others, like a pottery mould, are good for only one. If the pattern of consumers' demand changes (because of a change in fashion, say) some capital goods might be reused or adapted to serve the new purposes; but others might have to be scrapped. Producers' decisions will depend partly on how *convertible* the capital goods are to the new purposes.

Capital is an idea, not a thing

We need to remember that *capital* is just an *idea*, not a *thing*. Like 'size', it does not exist on its own, independent of the things we describe as large or small. Capital exists only in capital goods. Like other economic 'aggregates' (such as 'consumption' or 'national income') the mainstream (and Marxian) economists' use of 'capital' lumps together very different things. As a result, it disguises everything that is important: the precise *characteristics* of those different things, their *structure*, and their *meaning* for acting individuals.

It is confusion on this point which leads to the Marxian myth that capital 'reproduces itself' and 'hatches out profit'. Nothing could be more mistaken, says Mises. Capital does not grow out of thin air, only through the deliberate action of individuals who forgo consumption and create capital goods. It can be lost through mistakes, as when an entrepreneur misjudges the future market. It can even be consumed, as when people sell productive assets to pay their bills or boost their spending. It can also be wasted, as when governments subsidise investments that make no economic sense. So it is by no means self-reproducing.

Socialists often suggest they could transform a country's output by tearing down the old productive infrastructure and replacing it with one that is more modern and efficient. But capital takes time and trouble to accumulate: it has to be saved for, so cannot all be instantly replaced. Moreover, replacing existing capital assets would waste the time and trouble that has already been invested in them. It does not always make economic sense to do what is technologically feasible: people do not rush out and replace their vacuum cleaners, Mises notes, every time a new model comes out.

And socialist authorities are not necessarily the best placed to decide what sorts of capital goods should be acquired and how they should be used. In the market economy, *consumers* ultimately decide this through their spending choices. Under socialism, the decision has to be left to planners, who have no yardstick by which to measure the values of millions of disparate consumers.

The phenomenon of interest

Interest is a concept that is just as complicated, and just as human, as capital. *Market* interest rates include various elements, such as the profit of the lenders, a margin in case some borrowers default, and probably much more. But the basic element of interest – what Mises calls *originary interest* – encapsulates people's time preferences. In simple terms, would they prefer $100 now or $104, say, a year from now?

As always, the decision depends on the individuals involved. Capital is not something that automatically produces or 'yields' interest, just as trees yield fruit. In fact, the idea of 'capital' is just an abstract accounting tool: in reality, capital exists only in capital goods. And as we have seen, there is nothing automatic about capital goods producing a profit or an income.

Interest, then, is not a 'product' of capital. It arises only because people generally value present consumption more than future consumption. We cannot *abolish* interest, as some idealists suggest, because it is simply a part of human nature. Nor, in fact, would we want to abolish it: the prospect of enhanced consumption in the future is the incentive that tempts people to make the sacrifices that are needed to create capital goods, and so to raise human productivity.

Once again, it is individual values and choices which explain the phenomenon of interest. Since human beings do not live for ever, their actions are necessarily shaped by time preferences. Government attempts to manipulate (usually, to cap) interest rates are as misguided as trying to cap human emotions through force of law. The inevitable effect of interest-rate capping is to reduce the rewards that come from saving and investment, leading to lower savings, fewer capital goods being created and reduced future productivity.

9 MONEY AND INFLATION

Money is one of the most important elements of the market economy. Economic transactions depend on it. And once again, says Mises, we can understand its economic role and effects only if we understand its *meaning* to individuals.

Money as an exchange good

The nature of money always puzzled economists. It is not a production good: indeed, entrepreneurs have to *give it up* in order to acquire the capital goods they need to produce things. Nor is it a consumption good: people do not hold money simply for the joy of it – except, possibly, for a few pathological misers. So what exactly *is* money?

In a dazzling piece of analysis, Mises solved this puzzle.[1] Money, he argued, *is* an economic good, albeit a rather unusual one. Its purpose is neither production nor consumption. Its purpose is *exchange*. And the reason that people want to hold money is because it *facilitates the exchange* of other goods.

It is easy to see why. Without money, we would struggle to find people who had exactly the things we wanted and who were immediately willing to take exactly what we had to offer

---

1   See in particular *The Theory of Money and Credit* for his arguments on this.

in exchange. Hungry barbers would be scouring the country for bakers in need of haircuts. But through the medium of money, the barber can exchange a haircut for cash, then exchange that cash for bread from any baker at any time in the future.

The supply, demand and price of money

Like other economic goods, money is scarce and there is a *demand* for it. People want to own a store of it, to have it to hand so that they can exchange it for the goods they might need in the future.

And like other economic goods, money has a *price* – the rate at which it does in fact exchange with other things. This price is expressed a little oddly – not in terms of the volume of goods that will exchange for one unit of it (how many eggs to the dollar), but in terms of the number of units of money that exchange for another good (how many cents for an egg); and we do not usually talk about the 'price' of money, but its *purchasing power*. Yet it is a price like any other, based on the forces of supply and demand.

The *demand for money* depends upon the values of the individuals concerned. How much money people want to hold for the purpose of making future transactions will depend upon their temperament and their circumstances. Indeed, it is affected not just by how they value money as a medium of exchange, but on how they value the various other goods that they can buy with it. And this demand will affect the price, or the purchasing power, of money.

Money, in other words, is not something that stands outside markets. It is not some unchanging standard of prices. It in fact has a price of its own, determined by how the relevant individuals at the particular time and place value the services it provides.

The *money supply* is no less complex than the demand. There are different kinds of money. There is *commodity money*, such as gold and silver, which has commercial uses in addition to its use as a medium of exchange. There is what Mises calls *credit money*, such as the credit notes issued by banks against their reserves. And there is *fiat money*, the notes and coins produced by national governments, which are no longer claims on treasury reserves: they are just pieces of paper, or tokens, but they are nevertheless commonly accepted as a medium of exchange.

In fact, many of the things we call 'money' are just *money substitutes* – merely claims on money, says Mises, as a bread ticket is a claim on bread. They include banknotes and instant-access deposit accounts. But they are so convenient – saving us having to carry around exchangeable commodities like gold and silver – that we happily use and exchange them *as if* they were real money.

These complexities of supply and demand, shaped as they are by the values of the individuals involved, mean once again that simplistic models can be utterly misleading. The doctrine of *monetarism*, for example, suggests that an increase in the money supply causes a proportionate fall in the purchasing power of money: like most other goods, the price falls when there is more of it around. And in fact Mises accepts the general validity of this reasoning. But the precise outcome, he insists, is far from certain. What people think of the different kinds of money, for example, or of their different sources (governments, banks or agreement between traders), will colour how they value them and changes in them. Variations in the supply of different kinds of money and money substitutes – or in their relative balance – may produce quite unpredictable results.

Undermining the value of money

Sometimes, indeed, the results can be catastrophic. For instance, if the volume of money substitutes is expanded too far, comparable to there being many more bread tickets than there is bread (the so-called *fiduciary* issue), people may lose confidence that these paper claims will be honoured. That could well spark a run on a bank, or the collapse of a nation's currency.

Indeed, whatever their convenience, the ease with which some forms of money or money substitutes can be expanded is something that carries significant risks. The supply of a *commodity* money like gold or silver tends to be rather stable, although new discoveries or technologies (such as improved mining techniques) might boost it. But then the banks, or a country's central bank, can instantly increase the deposits in people's accounts at the stroke of a pen.

Under the prevailing 'fractional reserve' system, there are often legal or self-imposed limits on how far the banks can do this; but even so, the reserves in the banks' vaults can still be magnified several times through this method. There is even less restraint on the government, which can print new notes or create new bank deposits more or less as it pleases. With more money or money substitutes around, their price – that is, their purchasing power – will diminish. And this will show itself as a rise in the prices of other goods – what is commonly called *inflation*.[2]

---

2   To Mises, inflation is an over-expansion of money or credit itself, above the demand for it; but most people use the term to mean the general rise in prices that results.

The real consequences of monetary expansion

The simple monetarist view is that a surge in money or credit will have no lasting effects on the economy, apart from this purely 'nominal' increase in prices. Mises rejects this, arguing that the effects will be real – and damaging.

One reason is that no such expansion is uniform. It has to start somewhere; and from there it spreads out, affecting different people at different times. It may start with the government printing more notes, which allows it to buy more goods and services. Its suppliers will be the first to benefit, and with higher sales they will be able to raise wages and pay more for their own supplies. So their workers and suppliers will be the next to benefit; and so the boom spreads out from sector to sector. Like an avalanche, says Mises, prices and wages rise; real resources such as materials and labour are drawn in from one sector to the next, and to the next, and the next. The monetary change has caused real changes in how economic resources are allocated, not just 'nominal' changes in prices.

Even if the expansion *could* be made uniform, its effects on prices would be far from equal. Some individuals might choose to spend the increase, others may choose to save it. And more money going into people's pockets does not mean they will simply buy proportionately more of everything. They may well buy more luxuries and fewer of the low-quality basics. So again, the expansion is not neutral, but will have real effects on the pattern of consumption and production.

As the boom avalanches through the economy, some people will fare better than others. Those nearest the centre of the expansion will benefit most, while those last in line will probably suffer the effect of the widespread price rises long before they experience any direct benefit from the spreading boom. People's gains or losses will also depend in part upon how accurately they anticipate the price avalanche. Some people might suppose that the price rises are only temporary, and not change their spending habits; but as the price rises persist, they will be left worse off, since their cash buys them less and less. Others, sensing this, may do better by rushing out to spend their cash before its purchasing power falls even further.

If the price rises continue, though, more and more people will rush to spend their cash before it becomes worth even less. Spending will rise dramatically, but so will prices, and there is the risk that the boom will turn into what Mises calls a *crack-up boom* as people feverishly attempt to spend their devaluing currency until the whole monetary system breaks down under the pressure. He had, of course, seen exactly that in Europe in the 1920s.

The goals of monetary policy

The danger of such booms and busts is real. But there is always a temptation for governments to initiate such an expansion because, being at its centre, they are the first to gain, and they gain most.

How, then, should we arrange our monetary policy in order to prevent such expansions? Forcing governments to aim for a stable price level will not work, says Mises. There is no such thing as a price 'level' – different prices are rising and falling all the time. You can try to summarise price movements in a *price index* based on a particular basket of goods; but the result will depend on exactly what is put in the basket – and it will be the political authorities which decide.

In the past, Mises claims, state regulation of issuing banks, and government monopolies over note issuance, have been far less successful at delivering price stability than has uncontrolled private enterprise. So he sees the first duty of the authorities as being to affirm and support the choice of whatever monetary commodity is preferred by people in the marketplace. It might be gold, or silver, or something quite different; but whatever people choose, policy should aim to prevent it being corrupted for political purposes.

A commodity standard?

If we are to build a secure monetary system, Mises concludes, it would have to be based on such a commodity standard (such as gold); and all future issues of notes or bank deposits would have to be limited. He admits that a commodity standard is not ideal: there are costs in extracting and storing the commodity; its value still fluctuates according to changes in supply and demand; and we will still need some sort of paper certificate and accounting system to use it efficiently. But the key advantage of a commodity currency is that it would be independent of governments – or more specifically, of politicians seeking to buy popularity by engineering booms that, in the event, turn into damaging busts.

Nevertheless, there is little support today for the gold standard that Mises favoured and which many Austrian economists continue to favour. Politicians believe that their fiat currencies have generally served us well. Yes, there has been inflation, but, they argue, it is now better understood and so can be prevented. And yes, there have been the occasional downturns, some of them severe. But in the decades since we abandoned gold, the world economy has grown at an enormous pace.

For as long as it is widely believed that fiat currency is indeed helping the world economy expand in reasonable security, Mises is unlikely to win large numbers of people over to a gold standard. Even so, he still has much of value to say about the management of a nation's money today. In particular the idea of 'narrow banking' – in which there are strict limits on the volume of new money that the banks can create – owes much to Mises, and for all those who experienced the financial carnage that followed the huge expansion of bank credit in the years up to 2007, the policy does have a certain appeal.

10 THE TRAGEDY OF THE BUSINESS CYCLE

Economists have long speculated about why economic activity seems to swing cyclically, from periods of growth to periods of recession – the so-called *business cycle*. Earlier Austrian School economists had tackled the subject before Mises, and it was left to his colleague F. A. Hayek to publish the results of their joint work on the subject; so Mises has received little recognition for his own contribution. But that contribution was critical: in characteristic style, Mises unified several themes – money and credit, production processes, prices and interest rates – into a comprehensive theory of booms and slumps.[1]

Mises thought that money, in the broadest sense – including the fiduciary media of government notes, coins and uncovered banknotes and deposits – was the root of this particular evil. Monetary expansions affect relative prices and create real distortions. They also bring new funds surging on to the loan market, which bids down market interest rates. In turn, cheaper loans encourage entrepreneurs to borrow and build new and more sophisticated production processes. But as the boom washes through, he explained, this could all prove to be a costly mistake.

---

1 See *The Theory of Money and Credit*, and also *Human Action*.

The lure of cheap borrowing

The key indicator is what Mises calls *originary interest*. This is the interest rate that reflects people's actual time preferences – that they are prepared to wait a year to turn $100 worth of consumption into $104, say, as was explained earlier. If a production process can generate returns equal to or greater than this, then it makes economic sense. If it cannot, then the investment is not justified.

If the surge of new loan funds means that market interest rates are bid down below the originary rate, it becomes profitable to borrow to make investments that are not actually justified by people's time preferences. Entrepreneurs find themselves building new production processes that will ultimately fail. This is the root of the business cycle.

The progress of the business cycle

At first, with the surge of new funds making borrowing cheaper, everything looks promising for entrepreneurs. With cheaper borrowing, new production projects now appear more profitable. So entrepreneurs borrow to buy in materials and labour, and order new capital equipment. The boom has started.

Before long, though, competition between entrepreneurs for labour and materials will drive up wage rates and the prices of production goods. But then the higher wages of the workers will bid up the prices of consumption goods too. This again gives heart to entrepreneurs, who, despite rising costs, now at least anticipate a healthy price for their final product. So they carry on, and the boom continues.

Rising costs mean, however, that entrepreneurs have to

borrow even more to sustain their new production processes. They know that if they abandon their projects now, they will undoubtedly face losses. Like a builder who has oversized a set of foundations and run out of bricks, they borrow to keep building, hoping that their previous investment can be saved.

But unless the surge in loan funds continues, market interest rates will start to rise again, because entrepreneurs' demand for loans now outstrips the available supply. Entrepreneurs' budgets will be squeezed and they will be forced to cut back: wages will be cut, or workers laid off, and the boom will stall.

And this is exactly what does happen. The accelerating pace of borrowing that is needed to sustain the boom cannot continue indefinitely. Lenders start to worry about the security of the loans they have made and begin to rein back. But this new squeeze simply reveals the unsustainability of the original boom. Projects that cheap borrowing made profitable are now exposed as unprofitable.

The return to monetary stability does not *cause* the crisis: it merely brings to light the past investment mistakes. And those mistakes will lead to real losses. Unable to keep borrowing more and more, firms will run out of cash. They will have to sell assets for what they can get; factories will be closed, construction projects abandoned and workers dismissed. Firms will default on their loans, and lenders will raise interest rates even further to compensate, making it still harder for borrowers to survive. Even prudent firms will suffer from the credit crunch. As failures rise, the downswing descends into panic.

No painless escape

Politicians may claim that panic itself is the cause of the disaster, that all we have to fear is fear itself, and that if only we regained our confidence, it would halt the downward spiral. But Mises insists that this is not so. There is no way out of the unfolding process other than to let the effects of the past investment mistakes work themselves out.

In the meantime, capital will have been destroyed and consumers will have been left worse off by the episode. The money and credit boom has not enriched them, as its instigators hoped, but has impoverished them. In the process, the balance of wealth and income will have shifted; new patterns of spending power will have arisen, and new price relationships will have to be learnt and worked around. It will take time and effort to rebuild production to reflect the new patterns of consumer demand.

There is no way out of the process, says Mises, except to go through the dismal downswing of falling prices and wages. Any attempt to delay the adjustment – by trade unions or governments resisting lay-offs and wage cuts, for example – simply prolongs the agony and delays the eventual recovery. The sad fact is that the original, illusory boom did not herald the start of a new prosperity, but gulled businesses into wasting precious resources on bad investments. No subsequent efforts can change that historical fact, nor its malign effects.

The Mises–Hayek explanation today

The Keynesian economists who dominated the thinking in post-war Europe and America, of course, never accepted the explanation of business cycles put forward by Mises and Hayek.

They thought that downturns were a sign that further expansion was needed, not the inevitable legacy of past mistakes. That, of course, fuelled much of the high inflation of the 1960s and 1970s in particular. Even the monetarists who helped bring that inflation to heel did not accept the Austrian explanation. Milton Friedman, for example, concluded that it was 'contradicted by the evidence', and he believed it 'false'.

Interest in the Mises–Hayek view has resurged, however, following the financial crisis that (to non-Austrians at least) first manifested itself in 2007. For the events do seem to correspond with their analysis. For a decade and more, the UK and US monetary authorities in particular flooded their world with cheap credit. They kept interest rates low, seeing that as the only way to avoid downturns after confidence-shattering events such as the 1987 stock market crash, Russia's 1998 debt default or the September 2001 terrorist attacks in the USA. They also believed that millions of new Chinese savers coming into the world economy meant that interest rates should be lowered, just to reflect the realities of supply and demand. (In a free market, interest rates would find their own level, of course; but in this manipulated market, the authorities decide the price of credit.) And a third factor was that huge volumes of cheap goods coming in from China kept the prices of goods down and convinced the authorities that they were not over-expanding the supply of money.

They were, of course, and in the process they were stoking up a huge boom, as was particularly obvious in the housing market, where cheap loans fuelled an enormous rise in demand. Eventually the crunch came, as Mises and Hayek said it always does, and much of the developed world was plunged into recession as the investment mistakes of past years were written off. And Mises would see the UK and US response to the downturn – trying to buy themselves out by printing money and borrowing on an unprecedented scale – as simply debasing the currency, messing up markets and therefore delaying the eventual recovery.

11 THE PROBLEMS OF SOCIALISM

In interwar Europe, socialism seemed unstoppable. Many different varieties were on offer – international socialism, state socialism and the planned economy among them. But whatever the brand, the fundamental idea of socialism, according to Mises, is that all the means of production are in the exclusive control of the organised community.[1]

Consumption and production goods

Socialists, he says, focus on the common ownership of the means of production, because the idea of common ownership of other things is obvious nonsense. Ownership means having the power to dispose of something. You cannot call someone the *owner* of a house if they have no power to decide how it is used or whether it can be given or sold to someone else. Equal ownership would mean equal *control* or equal *use*.

But equal control or use of *consumption goods* – such as food, clothing, cars, pets, cigars, wristwatches – is impossible. Different people cannot wear the same coat at the same time. Two children can share a bar of chocolate, but only after it is divided up into different portions. The fact that even socialist countries use

---

1   This view is from his book *Omnipotent Government*, but the most comprehensive statement of the arguments is found in *Socialism*.

market structures to deliver such goods, and allow them to be bought and sold for exclusive use, is a clear indication of their non-collective nature.

Production goods seem quite different, however. They serve enjoyment only indirectly, being employed to produce consumption goods. Many people can benefit from them, without having to divide them up. They *can be* shared, and indeed *are* shared – by the shareholders of a quoted company, for example. So is socialism not just a matter of extending such joint ownership more widely, to everyone?

The socialist calculation problem

Hardly, says Mises. Modern productive investments are large, diverse and integrated. Somehow, we need to decide *which* of the many possible processes we should opt for. And even then we face a constant stream of future choices about *how* they are run, renewed and replaced. The snag for socialism is that we need some rational basis for making such complex decisions; but without prices and profits to guide investment, that presents a serious problem.

By the early 1900s, however, socialist intellectuals had come to see this problem as merely a technical one – a matter of solving a large number of simultaneous equations about supply and demand. But Mises showed that the *socialist calculation problem* was actually far deeper than this.

In the first place, there was a huge range of goods to be managed – not just physical plant and equipment, but semi-manufactured goods going through their different production processes; and labour has to be assigned too. Moreover, at every point in this hugely complex system, the decisions are not merely technical. They depend on how those involved *value* these different goods. But socialist planners cannot measure human values. Values are inherently personal. People disagree about them. So how are the planners to choose?

And the problem runs deeper still. To achieve one valued aim, we have to give up others. We might value the benefits of electricity, say, but should we produce it by mining more coal or by building a new hydroelectric dam? Whichever process we alight on, it will mean giving up time, land, labour and other resources that could have been used for some other purpose. Every production decision we take will affect countless others. And not everyone will agree on the choice anyway: environmentalists may value an undisturbed field or waterfall much more highly than the electric power derived from a new mine or dam.

The need for a unit of account

If we are to use resources rationally, then we need to make comparisons between them, and between the different products that emerge from their use. But the more complex the structure of production, the wider the choice of different processes and products that must be balanced. And the larger the number of people who will be affected, the more disagreement there will be, so the more difficult the decisions become.

We need, says Mises, some unit of account by which we can calculate whether an undertaking is sound or unsound. But there are no units that can measure different people's own valuations of different things. One person's values cannot be weighed against another's, any more than their grief, pain or happiness.

Calculation by money

In the free economy, there is a straightforward way in which we can get access to people's values – albeit indirectly. That is by examining the *actual* choices they make between one thing and another. We can measure how much of one thing they are in reality willing to give up for another – the rates of exchange between different goods that we call *prices*.

Market prices are a summary of the preferences of everyone engaged in the particular trade. And there are market prices for production and intermediate goods, as well as for consumption goods. Price allows us to reduce all the different economic choices that we need to make to a common unit: *money*.

Of course, money does not buy you love, or virtue, or sincerity. But it does indicate how much of one thing people will trade for another and so gives us a simple guide through the maze of *economic* possibilities.

Is it better to produce 1,000 litres of wine or 500 litres of oil? Without price, there is no common basis for calculating which we should produce, no data to feed a socialist planner's simultaneous equations. The choice would come down to the decision of some politician or official. It is a paradox of socialism that, because it abandons price, it necessarily replaces decision-making based on the choices of the whole community with the whim of a single individual or group.

Production goods without prices

Socialists might object that real-world socialist economies do not in fact abandon the use of money completely. Workers are still paid in money, and consumption goods are still bought and sold for cash. So there *is* a unit of account.

But under socialism, production goods are held in common ownership. They are never traded, never bought and sold, but continue as the joint property of the commonwealth. So prices are never established for them. Even if money is used elsewhere in the socialist economy, says Mises, it is still denied a role in production decisions.

This deficiency affects not just capital goods but all the goods involved in the production process. At any moment, thousands of production processes are going on. Only a few will produce finished consumption goods: most will produce capital goods and semi-manufactures. (As Carl Menger put it, every loaf of bread requires the production of flour, grain, ploughshares and iron ore.) At every stage in the life of these millions of intermediate products, managers must decide whether more work on them is justified and, if so, what. But without prices, there is no way to calculate the cost incurred in their production so far, or the cost of future possible stages of production. The whole economy becomes weakened by the lack of price information.

Calculations too large for the human mind

The aim of capitalist and socialist communities alike is to satisfy their citizens' most urgent needs. Capitalism does this constantly and systematically because it has a unit of calculation – *price* – based on people's actual choices. Under socialism, the process is far less direct. Someone has to decide what the public's needs are, which are most urgent, and how production is best steered to achieve them. But no planner can know what people truly value, and no amount of technology or mathematics can help in the matter. Technology and computation can tell us what we *can* achieve, but not what we *should* aim to achieve.

Even then, no human being could ever solve such complex production problems. Should a new railroad be constructed? What is the best route? Is the cost worth the transport and environmental benefits? What mix of skilled and unskilled labour is optimum? Could the fuel, iron and equipment be better used on other projects elsewhere? Without money, prices and profits, the mass of production possibilities is too bewildering for the human mind to cope with.

Things are even worse for the socialist planner, though, because even the basic information that you need for your calculations is impossible to collect. It is not just that economic conditions change rapidly and that, by the time information has been collected and transmitted to the planning centre, it is probably already out of date. The snag is more fundamental than that. As Hayek (building on the work of Mises) puts it, information about the realities of markets, and price movements, and demand, is inevitably local and *dispersed* through the economy. It is also inherently *subjective*: different people see only different parts of the picture; and their view may boil down to tacit understanding, instinct and experience, things that cannot actually be transmitted to another person – such as the central planner. Even if the planners had the finest calculating machine in the world, the information it would be working on would be incomplete, out of date and often contradictory.

Market socialism

One response to the calculation problem posed by Mises was 'market socialism'. Influential thinkers such as Oskar Lange and

Abba Lerner thought it possible to construct an 'ideal' market, with prices set by the administrators. Lerner suggested simple rules to guide managers – for example, that they should aim for output levels at which the prices of goods sold matched their production costs (meaning that the productive effort could not produce more value elsewhere).

Mises objected that this concept was far too static and theoretical. Perfection and balance can never exist in real-world economic processes, which are about the continual adjustment of complex, changing, diverse, interrelated events. Production choices can never be summarised or directed by simple rules.

Lange took the view that prices could be adjusted in response to any surpluses and shortages that arose, with managers told to adjust output accordingly. But Mises observes that this must be a very poor substitute for a genuine market economy, where countless entrepreneurs are constantly responding to even minute changes in supply and demand – and trying to anticipate the changes that will occur tomorrow.

Market socialism, it seems, will always be a step behind the real market economy. And socialism of any kind can survive only because there are real market economies around whose price relationships that it can copy. The dream of spreading socialism throughout the world would be self-defeating, says Mises. It would extinguish the last hope for rational economic calculation.

12 THE FLAWS IN MARXISM

To Mises, the core mistake of Marxism is just like the core mistake of mainstream economics. It sees human events as being determined by disembodied forces, rather than being shaped by the values and actions of individuals.[1]

An example is Marx's description of the 'stages' of economics and society. He argues that different technologies produce different sorts of social order. The agricultural age produced feudalism, while the industrial age produced the equally repressive capitalism. And the inevitable overthrow of capitalism will, at last, produce a liberating socialism.

Mises accepts that technological innovations can indeed free the human spirit – giving people the time and wealth for artistic and intellectual pursuits, for example. But that is not to say that all human society and human relationships are shaped solely by the prevailing productive technology. Usually, indeed, it is the other way round: values and institutions such as respect for property and security must be in place *before* capital goods can be built up; and the use of complicated production technology requires cooperation through specialisation and exchange. In other words, the social relations necessarily come first.

---

1   This critique of Marxism is spread across several books, including *Human Action*, *Socialism*, *Theory and History* and *The Ultimate Foundation of Economic Science*.

The supposed problems of capitalism

The same error pervades Marx's argument that capitalism must inevitably poison itself. To survive the cut-throat competition and maintain their own lifestyle, he explains, rich industrialists have to keep forcing down the wages of their workers. But by doing so, they impoverish the very customers on whom their businesses depend. Meanwhile, the same dog-eat-dog competition forces businesses to grow larger and larger as they strive to capture economies of scale and keep cutting costs. Eventually, competition is replaced by monopoly.

Mises objects that Marx completely forgets that businesses survive only by serving their customers; and the whole purpose of big business is to serve the masses. Ignoring the needs of these sovereign consumers would spell disaster for any firm. And in fact, far from grinding the masses into poverty, capitalism has always brought them material improvements. Marx, his mind prejudiced by a malign classism, has simply failed to grasp this harmony of objectives.

Ideology and class

But classism was vital to Marx: he was able to deflect all criticism merely by branding the critics as members of a hostile, self-promoting class whose minds were closed. Only in a classless socialist society would true enlightenment dawn.

This is nonsense, insists Mises. Even if 'bourgeois' economics *had* been devised solely to undermine feudalism and bolster capitalism, this does not necessarily make it *wrong*. And the bourgeois class would still be better served by adopting ideas that were *right* rather than ideas that were ideologically blinkered.

In any case, ideas do not immutably reflect group allegiances: Marx himself was (by our standards) definitely middle-class and his sponsor Engels was an industrialist. And class interests are not monolithic: free trade might benefit capitalists as a group, but individual capitalists might still campaign for import controls in their own specific sector. Meanwhile, some proletarians might argue that private ownership of production would serve their class better than communal ownership under socialism. But there can be no rational discussion about the matter when Marx and his followers have already decided that only fools or class traitors could possibly hold such views.

Marxism and classical economics

Mainstream economists find Marxism hard to critique, says Mises, precisely because they make the same mistake of treating economics as the interplay of impersonal forces, rather than the actions and values of individuals.

The Marxian idea that capitalism tends to monopoly is a case in point. The mainstream model of 'perfect competition', with its identical products and traders, is a bizarre oversimplification: but compound it with the commonsense view that large-scale production is always cheaper and it is only a short step to the conclusion that businesses must grow and grow until competition is forced out. But the real world is quite different. No products or traders are identical: there is a vast number of gradations in the quality, price and location of products, and as many different preferences as there are buyers and sellers. That enables small specialist firms to do good business by exploiting niche markets, while innovators can quickly whittle away the market of even the most established firm.

There is, therefore, no impersonal 'force' driving capitalism towards monopoly, and nothing inevitable about its replacement by socialism. Economics and politics are rooted in the choices of individual human beings, whose actions cannot be so easily predicted. It is a dangerous conceit to believe otherwise.

The erosion of freedom under socialism

If socialism means that the productive resources are owned by society, how does society then use and control them? Once again, Mises argues, Marxians overlook the human element. They talk glibly about the 'unitary will of society' as if 'society' were a creature with a mind of its own.

And they never specify how 'society' might actually express this 'will'. There is a reason for that, says Mises: the unpalatable truth that it would necessarily require some organ of *control*. Even committed socialists will argue over what should be done and how. Indeed, the disputes will be particularly severe, since the very organisation of society itself is at stake. Some people will remain vehemently opposed to whatever is decided. They – plus shirkers, and others who flout the collective decisions for their own gain – will somehow have to be brought into line.

Marxians may extol the 'unitary will' of society and the 'withering away of the state', but the non-existence of the first makes a pipedream of the second. To suppress any deviation from the common purpose, there will necessarily have to be some supreme authority, with coercive power – in other words, a *state*. It hardly matters what it is called or how it is constituted. The point, says Mises, is that it must have complete control. If the will of the majority is to prevail, there can be no room for dissent. Orders must be issued and obeyed. Even the choice of one's home and place of work must be surrendered. And with such potentially corrupting power vested in the supreme authorities, we should not be surprised when our other personal freedoms go the same way.

13 INTERVENTIONISM AND BUREAUCRACY

To Mises, then, socialism – public ownership of the means of production to advance material welfare – cannot work in practice and lacks any coherent theoretical foundation too. The fall of the Berlin Wall in 1989 certainly exposed how right Mises had been about the economic calculation problem. It was obvious to any Westerner that the Soviet bloc's resources were massively misallocated: factories were miles from their markets, machines were hugely over-engineered, metals and other commodities were being squandered, even as basic human needs went unmet. Enormous restructuring was inevitable.

With this painful reality still live in people's minds, few who call themselves socialists today want to recreate a world of wholesale state ownership. Rather, they argue that private industry must be heavily regulated, so that the energy and discipline of the market can be directed to serve and maximise the welfare of the entire community – however they define it.

Yet although his arguments on socialism aimed at a target that has now long since been whisked away, Mises has still left us with plenty of arguments that explain why this approach is just as incoherent and impractical as full-blown socialism. In his critique of what he calls *interventionism*, he gives us a very useful and apposite critique of modern 'third way' thinking.

Hostility against capitalism

Why are so many people still hostile to capitalism? Partly, Mises suspects, it is precisely because success or failure in the market is driven by the free choices of individual consumers. Their money 'votes' go to those who bring them most satisfaction; they care little about other people's view of their own self-worth.

Intellectuals, who think they should be at the top of the tree, for example, are not always or automatically well rewarded in the market system. They may resent the fact that they are paid less than many unskilled workers and regard it as unfair. In market terms, though, the difference may be perfectly justified: people dislike dirty, dangerous or menial jobs, and may well demand high wages to take them.

But the market system is about the satisfaction of consumers' needs for goods and services. It does not exist to promote particular groups, or even particular virtues and values. However much resentment any group may feel, says Mises, their wages cannot long be held above the market level without causing the worse evil of unemployment. Our dreams of what an ideal world might look like cannot change the logic of economic science.

Misguided efforts to improve capitalism

Indeed, our efforts to manipulate the market economy, and make it conform to a particular vision, are invariably damaging. Capitalism is superbly good at boosting the general standard of living by encouraging people to specialise and build up the capital goods that raise the productivity of human effort. But when we tax or regulate this system, and make it less worthwhile to invest in and own capital goods, then capitalism can falter. But that is not a 'crisis of capitalism', explains Mises. It is a crisis of interventionism: a failure of policies that are intended to 'improve' capitalism but in fact strangle it.[1]

One common political ideal, for example, is 'economic democracy' – the idea that everyone should count in the production and allocation of economic goods, not just a few capitalist producers. But according to Mises, we already *have* economic democracy. In competitive markets, producers are necessarily ruled by the wishes of consumers. Unless they satisfy the demands of consumers, they will lose trade and go out of business. If we interfere in this popular choice, we will end up satisfying only the agenda of some particular political group.

A more modest notion is that producers' profits should be taxed so that they can be distributed more widely throughout the population. But while this shares out the rewards of success, says Mises, it leaves business burdened with the whole cost of failure. That is an imbalance that can only depress people's willingness to take business risks and must thereby depress economic life itself.

No progress without private property

The important thing to remember is that wealth does not come naturally. It has to be *created*, and it is created only by *people* who are prepared to save and forgo consumption in order to accumulate productive capital goods. Capital takes effort to build up, and people will not make that effort unless they enjoy its rewards. Indeed, capital that has already been built up can be very easily destroyed, dissipated and wasted. If we reduce the incentives for

---

1   For the full arguments outlined in this chapter, see *A Critique of Interventionism*, *Socialism* and *Bureaucracy*.

people to create and enjoy capital, we will not produce a more just or equal world, just a poorer one.

The respect for personal property, therefore, is crucial to Mises. Capitalism is not just about *allocating* resources: it actually *creates* resources that never existed before. And it is only *because* we have rules to protect the ownership and enjoyment of those things that our standard of living has been able to grow so far and so fast.

Interventionism

Many people think that, through government intervention, we can improve capitalism without going so far as full socialism. Mises is less confident.

Markets are complicated: interfering with them at one point produces side effects – often, very unwelcome side effects – at another, he observes. A government might aim to create jobs by spending on public works, for example. If the money comes from taxes, that raises costs for businesses, and so destroys as many jobs as it creates. If it comes from borrowing, that leads to credit expansion and inflation – which also destroys jobs. So the authorities will find themselves drawn into yet further interventions in order to try to correct these new problems. And in this way, the pattern repeats. Eventually, although the economy still *looks* capitalist, it ends up being completely controlled by the authorities.

Price and wage controls

A common form of interventionism is *price controls* on essential goods that the authorities deem 'too expensive'. Mises takes the example of a government order to set maximum prices for milk, aiming to make milk more affordable to poor families. Unfortunately, the lower price encourages people to buy more milk; but it makes milk production less attractive. Some producers may even start to lose money and quit the business. With demand higher and production shrinking, there will not be enough milk to go round. Now even the poor may get less milk than they had before.

In response, the government might try rationing milk to ensure that needy groups get their share. Or it might set limits on the price of animal fodder, hoping to keep down farmers' costs. But then fodder production goes the same way as milk production. Or a whole bureaucracy of rationing is created. Once again, the effort to control just one thing has led to a huge structure of restraints.

Another common intervention, aimed at helping the working poor, is to set *minimum wage rates*. But higher wages raise businesses' costs. To stay in business they will have to lay off workers, or raise their prices to consumers – which will reduce demand for their product and so precipitate lay-offs too. The higher and more extensive that minimum wages are, the wider and deeper is the unemployment they create.

Once again, the government will be pressured to intervene, perhaps with new rules making it harder to fire workers, or new taxes to fund social benefits. But these just impose even more costs on businesses and so deepen the problem.

Bureaucracy

One reason why capitalism is so much more efficient than interventionism or socialism is that business has one clear aim – to make a profit – and that it is easy to see whether this single objective has been met. The aims of a public enterprise, by contrast, are much more diffuse, says Mises. It is expected to provide a range of 'socially necessary' or 'essential' or 'desirable' services – but there is no obvious way of measuring its success on delivering or balancing these vague objectives.

How, for example, should we measure the output of a police force? Different people, with different concerns, will probably judge it in quite different ways. So how can we decide whether such an agency is providing good value for money? Or is over-staffed? Or is even necessary?

What happens, says Mises, is that because outputs are so hard to define, agency managers come to be controlled instead by an overlay of rules on their actions and spending. But then they become mere bureaucrats who have to ask higher authorities before they can do anything new.

Effects and lack of a solution

Plainly, this makes public agencies much less flexible than private enterprises. In the market, a single individual can take risks and pioneer a completely new way of doing things, such as a new process that raises quality and cuts costs. But public agency managers have limited discretion; inevitably they lag behind changing technologies and events.

Even their hiring of personnel is less efficient and less focused on the needs of the general public. In the competitive world of the marketplace, entrepreneurs have to hire the people they know will do the best job for their customers – not just people they happen to like. Bureaucratic careers, by contrast, are based on the personal judgements of superiors, says Mises, and patronage is rife.

There is no solution to these problems. They stem from the vagueness of the objectives imposed on public bodies. And it is no good entreating government officials to act 'entrepreneurially'. The objectives of the commercial firm and the bureaucracy are wholly different. They have different ways of working and need different management methods. Even bringing in managers from business does not help: their accounting and management skills are simply inappropriate to the task. The belief that state institutions can improve on the market by taking what it does and somehow doing it better is plainly a dangerous conceit.

14 THE LIBERAL ALTERNATIVE

Living in interwar Europe, Mises saw some of the worst effects of nationalism, and hated it. One of its roots, he thought, was interventionism, which inevitably requires import and migration controls to protect itself. Measures to keep wages high or profits high, for example, will be undermined if cheap labour and goods can flood in from abroad. But those same barriers, he argues, promote hostility among the outsiders, raise tensions, and often spark conflicts.[1]

Capitalism, however, gives a much smaller role to the state and requires trade, not protectionism, to operate successfully. Indeed, Mises explains (though the argument is not original to him), the more free and open that trade is, the better it works. And when nations are mutually dependent on trade with each other, war becomes unthinkable. Durable peace, he concludes, is possible only under a thoroughgoing, liberal capitalism.

Mises was not entirely right that trading partners do not go to war; indeed, this is more common than any type of conflict. But there is no doubt that the interests of the individual citizens of any country are best served by maintaining peaceful relationships with their trading partners. Perhaps the apparent contradiction simply illustrates another point made often by Mises – that

---

1   See in particular *Nation, State, and Economy* for the explanation of this.

the interests of the politicians are often starkly different from the interests of the general public.

The liberal framework

Nevertheless, the main reason to prefer liberalism as a social order, says Mises, is that it *works*.[2] It limits conflicts between groups and promotes voluntary cooperation between individuals. The great nineteenth-century era of free trade and deregulation, for example, produced a surge in productivity and a rise in living standards that spread right throughout the growing population.

Yet it can be hard to win support for liberalism. Its greatest benefit – that, in the long run, the whole population is enriched through more freedom in commerce – is less obvious to people than the immediate gains that result from intervention. Liberalism does not even promise to win privileges for its own supporters: its object is to improve life for everybody.

Nor does liberalism aim to produce a particular social structure or a particular distribution of income. It merely establishes a *framework* of peace, stability and equality before the law, and within that framework, people are free to cooperate in any way they see fit. Liberalism does not say what should be produced, or how much, or by whom. These things are merely the *outcome* of the complex, voluntary interactions between free individuals.

Mises maintains that the liberal framework will produce peaceful and efficient cooperation between individuals and groups. Under liberalism, our differences are not a potential source of conflict but a potential opportunity to trade. The more

---

2   The full case for the liberal approach can be found in *Liberalism*, and to some extent in *Economic Policy*.

that people disagree on the value of something, the more they each gain by exchanging it. And exchange allows us to specialise and use our different abilities to our advantage, and so to share in the task of creating things that would be beyond the capabilities of any single individual.

The underpinnings of a liberal order

To Mises, the role of the liberal state is not to force individuals to act in particular ways, but to maintain the framework that enables them to cooperate, while maximising the sphere of voluntary action and minimising the need for coercion. Three things are vital to maintaining this framework, he says: peace, freedom and property.

Peace is essential because economic actions, such as investments in new productive processes, require us to take decisions based on assumptions about the future. A state of war makes the future impossible to predict. Farmers, for example, cannot plant crops with confidence if there is a strong risk of their crops being destroyed or their land being confiscated by hostile forces.

Freedom is essential because people cannot make rational economic choices if others tell them how to act. And in any case, people who work on their own volition are incomparably more productive than slaves who are forced to work for someone else.

Property is essential if the system of specialisation and trade is to flourish. If people are to save and invest in capital goods, they need to know that their investment is secure and that they can enjoy the fruits of that effort.

The benefits of liberalism

The fact that liberalism depends so much on the institution of private property may suggest that it would most benefit the rich and acquisitive. Mises utterly rejects this. To him, private property is an essential condition for efficient production and the higher living standards that specialisation can deliver. But under liberalism, people are not forced to pursue material wealth: they can, and do, pursue many other things. And even those who do not own property will still benefit from the generally rising living standards that liberalism creates, and the opportunities that open up when privileges and controls are ended.

Under capitalism, it is the mass of consumers who are sover eign, not the rich. Producers cannot force their products on to anyone: consumers take them only if they choose to. It is no coincidence that the age of capitalism has been the age of mass production. It has made access to decent food, clothing and shelter available to everyone, not just the rich: even luxuries like cars and televisions are now taken for granted. The reality of capitalism contrasts starkly with Marx's prediction that it would drive workers' wages down to subsistence levels.

Liberalism empowers the general population in another important way. It gives them the ability to plan. Planning, says Mises, is not something restricted to central authorities: we all plan. The choice is not between planning and no planning, but *whose* plan prevails. And since only *individuals* can know their own needs, aims and values, especially in a fast-moving economy, Mises thinks it far better to let individuals plan for themselves.

Liberalism and equality

Nevertheless, the fact that liberalism does not promise income equality makes some critics worry about the fate of those who end up poor. Mises regards this fear as misplaced. The working poor in today's advanced economies are incomparably better off, he says, than those in pre-capitalist societies, who must eke a self-sufficient living out of the land – if they have land.

In capitalism, though, almost anyone can find a productive niche that serves others and so brings at least some reward. If not, families and charities can provide. Critics may argue that charity is not up to this task: but the greatest surge in philanthropy, says Mises, has occurred under capitalism. With the rising living standards that capitalism brings, there is more wealth to spare for charity; and even those on modest incomes become better able to protect themselves with insurance. It is *interventionism* which eats up people's capital and leaves charitable institutions poorer – which, of course, brings spiralling demands for more intervention in the form of welfare support.

Critics misunderstand the nature of inequality under liberalism, which is quite different from inequality in the pre-capitalist world. In the market society, wealth is not a privilege, but comes only through benefiting consumers. And it lasts only as long as producers continue to provide those benefits.

Moreover, the luxuries that rich people enjoy are not permanently closed off to the rest of us. The market economy is dynamic. All innovations – cars, sanitation, electricity – begin as luxuries for the well off, says Mises: but before long they become 'necessities' for all.

But then, that steady rise in the wellbeing of all humanity must, surely, be the primary goal of economic policy, and the

reason why we need to understand the true nature and ultimate
foundation of economic science.

15 QUOTATIONS FROM LUDWIG VON MISES

On the problems of socialism

The essence of socialism is this: all the means of production are in the exclusive control of the organized community. This and this alone is socialism. All other definitions are misleading.

Socialism, p. 239

The experiences of a remote and bygone period of simple production do not provide any sort of argument for establishing the possibility of an economic system without monetary calculation.

Economic calculation in the socialist commonwealth, p. 103

Without the basis for calculation which capitalism places at the disposal of socialism, in the shape of market prices, socialist enterprises would never be carried on, even within single branches of production or individual countries.

Socialism, p. 136

All economic change ... would involve operations the value of which could neither be predicted beforehand nor ascertained after they had taken place. Everything would be a leap in the dark. Socialism is the renunciation of rational economy.

Socialism, p. 122

The human mind cannot orientate itself properly among the bewildering mass of products and potentialities of production ... It would simply stand perplexed ...

*Economic calculation in the
socialist commonwealth*, p. 103

Many popular fallacies concerning socialism are due to the mistaken belief that all friends of socialism advocate the same system ... If a man says socialism, or planning, he always has in view his own brand of socialism, his own plan. Thus planning does not in fact mean preparedness to co-operate peacefully. It means conflict.

Omnipotent Government, p. 243

The socialist community is a great authoritarian association in which orders are issued and obeyed. This is what is implied by the words 'planned economy' and the 'abolition of the anarchy of production'.

Socialism, p. 185

On the dangers of interventionism

The idea that there is a *third* system – between socialism and capitalism, as its supporters say – a system as far away from socialism as it is from capitalism but retains the advantages and avoids the disadvantages of each – is pure nonsense.

Economic Policy, p. 51

The middle-of-the-road policy is not an economic system that can last. It is a method for the realization of socialism by installments.

Planning for Freedom, pp. 32–3

Representative democracy cannot subsist if a great part of the voters are on the government payroll.

Bureaucracy, p. 81

The public firm can nowhere maintain itself in free competition with the private firm; it is possible today only where it has a monopoly that excludes competition.

Nation, State, and Economy, p. 186

Such is the true story of modern monopoly. It is not an outcome of unhampered capitalism and of an inherent trend of capitalist evolution, as the Marxians would have us believe. It is, on the contrary, the result of government policies aiming at a reform of market economy.

Omnipotent Government, p. 72

[T]he science of economics proves with cold, irrefutable logic that the ideals of those who condemn making a living on the market are quite vain, that the socialist organization of society is quite unrealizable, that the interventionist order is nonsensical and contrary to the ends at which it aims, and that therefore the market economy is the only feasible system of social co-operation.

Epistemological Problems of Economics, p. 196

On liberalism

In the market economy, everyone serves his fellow citizens by serving himself. This is what the liberal authors of the Eighteenth Century had in mind when they spoke of the harmony of the rightly understood interests of all groups and of all individuals of the population.

Economic Policy, p. 23

In an age in which nations are mutually dependent on products of foreign provenance, war can no longer be waged.

Liberalism, p. 107

This is the function that the liberal doctrine assigns the state: the protection of property, liberty, and peace.

Liberalism, p. 37

The defence of a nation's security and civilization against aggression on the part both of foreign foes and domestic gangsters is the first duty of any government. If all men were pleasant and virtuous, no one coveted what belongs to another, there would be no need for a government, for armies and navies, for policemen, for courts, and prisons.

Bureaucracy, p. 24

On the drivers of economic progress

The profit motive is the means of making the public supreme. The better a man succeeds in supplying the consumer, the greater become his earnings. It is to everybody's advantage that the entrepreneur who produces shoes at the cheapest cost becomes rich; most people would suffer if a law were to limit his right to get richer.

Bureaucracy, p. 88

Liberalism champions private property in the means of production because it expects a higher standard of living from such an economic organization, not because it wishes to help the owners.

Socialism, p. 57

In the United States today the difference between a rich man and a poor man means very often only the difference between a Cadillac and a Chevrolet.

Economic Policy, p. 9

The philosophy underlying the system of progressive taxation is that the income and wealth of the well-to-do classes can be freely tapped. What the advocates of those tax rates fail to realize is that the greater part of the incomes taxed away would not have been consumed, but saved and invested. In fact, this fiscal policy does not only prevent the further accumulation of new capital. It brings about capital decumulation.

Planning for Freedom, p. 32

On the importance of individual values

Value is not intrinsic, it is not in things. It is within us; it is the way in which man reacts to the conditions of his environment.

Human Action, p. 96

Valuing is man's emotional reaction to the various states of his environment, both that of the external world and that of the physiological conditions of his own body.

The Ultimate Foundations of Economic Science, p. 37

Economics is not about things and tangible material objects; it is about men, their meanings and actions. Goods, commodities and wealth and all the other notions of conduct are not elements of nature; they are elements of human meaning and conduct. He who wants to deal with them must not look at the external world; he must search for them in the meaning of acting men.

Human Action, p. 92

We do not know why and how definite conditions of
the external world arouse in the human mind a definite
reaction. We do not know why different people and
the same people at different instants of their lives react
differently to the same external stimuli.

Theory and History, p. 69

The economists who want to substitute 'quantitative
economics' for what they call 'qualitative economics' are
utterly mistaken. There are, in the field of economics, no
constant relations, and consequently, no measurements
are possible ... Different individuals value the same things
in a different way, and valuations change with the same
individuals with changing conditions.

Human Action, pp. 55–6

On entrepreneurship and competition

Every action is a speculation, *i.e.* guided by a definite
opinion concerning the uncertain conditions of the future.
Even in short-run activities this uncertainty prevails.
Nobody can know whether some unexpected fact will not
render vain all that he has provided for the next day or the
next hour.

The Ultimate Foundations of Economic Science, p. 51

[T]housands of business people are trying day and night to
find some new product which satisfies the consumer better
or is less expensive to produce, or better *and* less expensive
than the existing products. They do not do this out of
altruism, they do it because they want to make money.

Economic Policy, p. 36

The development of capitalism consists in everyone having the right to serve the customer better and/or more cheaply. And this method, this principle, has, within a comparatively short time, transformed the whole world.

Economic Policy, p. 5

There is nothing automatic or mysterious about the operation of the market. The only forces determining the continually fluctuating state of the market are the value judgements of the various individuals and their actions as directed by these value judgements. The ultimate factor in the market is the striving of each man to satisfy his needs and wants in the best possible way.

Planning for Freedom, pp. 72–3

The market is not a place; it is a *process*, it is the way in which, by buying and selling, by producing and consuming, the individuals contribute to the total workings of society.

Economic Policy, p. 17

The sharper the competition, the better it serves its social function to improve economic production.

A Critique of Interventionism, p. 84

[T]here can be no question whatever of a tendency for fortunes to grow bigger and bigger. Fortunes cannot grow; someone has to increase them.

Socialism, p. 380

There are no means by which the general standard of living can be raised other than by accelerating the increase of capital as compared with population.

Planning for Freedom, pp. 5–6

On inflation, booms and busts

What is needed for a sound expansion of production is additional capital goods, not money or fiduciary media. The credit expansion is built on the sands of banknotes and deposits. It must collapse.

Human Action, p. 561

True, governments can reduce the rate of interest in the short run ... issue additional paper currency ... open the way to credit expansion by the banks. They can thus create an artificial boom and the appearance of prosperity. But such a boom is bound to collapse soon or late and to bring about a depression.

Omnipotent Government, p. 251

When people talk of a 'price level' they have in mind the image of a level of liquid which goes up or down according to the increase or decrease in its quantity, but which, like a liquid in a tank, rises evenly. But with prices, there is no such thing as a 'level'. Prices do not change to the same extent at the same time.

Economic Policy, p. 59

[T]he return to monetary stability does not *generate* a crisis. It only brings to light the malinvestments and other mistakes that were made under the hallucination of the illusory prosperity created by the easy money.

Planning for Freedom, p. 156

[T]he gold standard has one tremendous virtue: the quantity of the money supply, under the gold standard, is independent of the policies of governments and political parties.

Economic Policy, p. 65

SELECTED BOOKS AND ARTICLES BY MISES

The Theory of Money and Credit (1953), trans. H. E. Batson,
London: Jonathan Cape. Originally published in German in
1912 as *Theorie des Geldes und der Umlaufsmittel.*

Nation, State, and Economy (1988), trans. Leland B. Yeager, New
York: New York University Press. Originally published in
German in 1919 as *Nation, Staat, und Wirtschaft.*

'Economic calculation in the socialist commonwealth' (1935),
trans. S. Adler, reprinted in F. A. Hayek, *Collectivist Economic
Planning*, London: Routledge & Kegan Paul. Originally
published in German in 1920 as 'Die Wirtschaftsrechnung im
Sozialistischen Gemeinwesen'.

Socialism: An Economic and Sociological Analysis (1936), trans.
J. Kahane, London: Jonathan Cape. Originally published in
German in 1922 as *Die Gemeinwirtschaft: Untersuchungen über
den Sozialismus.*

Liberalism or *The Free and Prosperous Commonwealth: An
Exposition of the Ideas of Classical Liberalism* (1962), trans.
Ralph Raico, Princeton, NJ: D. Van Nostrand. Originally
published in German in 1927 as *Liberalismus.*

Monetary Stabilization and Cyclical Policy (1978), trans.
Bettina Bien Greaves, Dobbs Ferry, NY: Free Market

Books. Originally published in German in 1928 as
Geldwertstabilisierung und Konjunkturpolitik.

A Critique of Interventionism (1977), trans. Hans F. Sennholz, New
Rochelle, NY: Arlington House. Originally published in 1929
as *Kritik des Interventionismus.*

Epistemological Problems of Economics (1960), trans. George
Reisman, Princeton, NJ: D. Van Nostrand. Originally
published in German in 1933 as *Grundprobleme der
Nationalökonomie: Untersuchungen über Verfahren, Aufgaben,
und Inhalt der Wirtschafts und Gesellschaftslehre.*

Interventionism: An Economic Analysis (1998), trans. Bettina
Bien Greaves, Irvington-on-Hudson, NY: Foundation for
Economic Education. Excerpted from an original publication
in German in 1940, *Nationalökonomie: Theorie des Handelns
und Wirtschaftens.*

Omnipotent Government: The Rise of the Total State and Total War
(1944), New Haven, CT: Yale University Press.

Bureaucracy (1944), New Haven, CT: Yale University Press.

'Planning for freedom' (1945), in *Economic Planning*, New York:
Dynamic America. Reprinted in *Planning for Freedom,
and Other Essays and Addresses* (1952), South Holland, IL:
Libertarian Press.

Planned Chaos (1947), Irvington-on-Hudson, NY: Foundation for
Economic Education.

Human Action: A Treatise on Economics (1949), New Haven, CT:
Yale University Press.

The Anti-Capitalistic Mentality (1956), Princeton, NJ: D. Van
Nostrand.

*Theory and History: An Interpretation of Social and Economic
Evolution* (1957), New Haven, CT: Yale University Press.

The Ultimate Foundation of Economic Science: An Essay on Method (1962), Princeton, NJ: D. Van Nostrand.

The Historical Setting of the Austrian School of Economics (1969), New Rochelle, NY: Arlington House.

Notes and Recollections (1978), South Holland, IL: Liberation Press.

On the Manipulation of Money and Credit (1978), trans. Bettina Bien Greaves, Dobbs Ferry, NY: Free Market Books.

Economic Policy: Thoughts for Today and Tomorrow (1979), Chicago, IL: Regnery Gateway. (A collection of lectures given by Mises in South America in 1958.)

ABOUT THE IEA

The Institute is a research and educational charity (No. CC 235 351), limited by guarantee. Its mission is to improve understanding of the fundamental institutions of a free society by analysing and expounding the role of markets in solving economic and social problems.

The IEA achieves its mission by:

- a high-quality publishing programme
- conferences, seminars, lectures and other events
- outreach to school and college students
- brokering media introductions and appearances

The IEA, which was established in 1955 by the late Sir Antony Fisher, is an educational charity, not a political organisation. It is independent of any political party or group and does not carry on activities intended to affect support for any political party or candidate in any election or referendum, or at any other time. It is financed by sales of publications, conference fees and voluntary donations.

In addition to its main series of publications the IEA also publishes a quarterly journal, *Economic Affairs*.

The IEA is aided in its work by a distinguished international Academic Advisory Council and an eminent panel of Honorary Fellows. Together with other academics, they review prospective IEA publications, their comments being passed on anonymously to authors. All IEA papers are therefore subject to the same rigorous independent refereeing process as used by leading academic journals.

IEA publications enjoy widespread classroom use and course adoptions in schools and universities. They are also sold throughout the world and often translated/reprinted.

Since 1974 the IEA has helped to create a worldwide network of 100 similar institutions in over 70 countries. They are all independent but share the IEA's mission.

Views expressed in the IEA's publications are those of the authors, not those of the Institute (which has no corporate view), its Managing Trustees, Academic Advisory Council members or senior staff.

Members of the Institute's Academic Advisory Council, Honorary Fellows, Trustees and Staff are listed on the following page.

The Institute gratefully acknowledges financial support for its publications programme and other work from a generous benefaction by the late Alec and Beryl Warren.

Other papers recently published by the IEA include:

A Market in Airport Slots
Keith Boyfield (editor), David Starkie, Tom Bass & Barry Humphreys
Readings 56; ISBN 0 255 36505 5; £10.00

Money, Inflation and the Constitutional Position of the Central Bank
Milton Friedman & Charles A. E. Goodhart
Readings 57; ISBN 0 255 36538 1; £10.00

railway.com
Parallels between the Early British Railways and the ICT Revolution
Robert C. B. Miller
Research Monograph 57; ISBN 0 255 36534 9; £12.50

The Regulation of Financial Markets
Edited by Philip Booth & David Currie
Readings 58; ISBN 0 255 36551 9; £12.50

Climate Alarmism Reconsidered
Robert L. Bradley Jr
Hobart Paper 146; ISBN 0 255 36541 1; £12.50

Government Failure: E. G. West on Education
Edited by James Tooley & James Stanfield
Occasional Paper 130; ISBN 0 255 36552 7; £12.50

Corporate Governance: Accountability in the Marketplace
Elaine Sternberg
Second edition
Hobart Paper 147; ISBN 0 255 36542 x; £12.50

The Land Use Planning System
Evaluating Options for Reform
John Corkindale
Hobart Paper 148; ISBN 0 255 36550 0; £10.00

Economy and Virtue
Essays on the Theme of Markets and Morality
Edited by Dennis O'Keeffe
Readings 59; ISBN 0 255 36504 7; £12.50

Free Markets Under Siege
Cartels, Politics and Social Welfare
Richard A. Epstein
Occasional Paper 132; ISBN 0 255 36553 5; £10.00

Unshackling Accountants
D. R. Myddelton
Hobart Paper 149; ISBN 0 255 36559 4; £12.50

The Euro as Politics
Pedro Schwartz
Research Monograph 58; ISBN 0 255 36535 7; £12.50

Pricing Our Roads
Vision and Reality
Stephen Glaister & Daniel J. Graham
Research Monograph 59; ISBN 0 255 36562 4; £10.00

The Role of Business in the Modern World
Progress, Pressures, and Prospects for the Market Economy
David Henderson
Hobart Paper 150; ISBN 0 255 36548 9; £12.50

Public Service Broadcasting Without the BBC?
Alan Peacock
Occasional Paper 133; ISBN 0 255 36565 9; £10.00

The ECB and the Euro: the First Five Years
Otmar Issing
Occasional Paper 134; ISBN 0 255 36555 1; £10.00

Towards a Liberal Utopia?
Edited by Philip Booth
Hobart Paperback 32; ISBN 0 255 36563 2; £15.00

The Way Out of the Pensions Quagmire
Philip Booth & Deborah Cooper
Research Monograph 60; ISBN 0 255 36517 9; £12.50

Black Wednesday
A Re-examination of Britain's Experience in the Exchange Rate Mechanism
Alan Budd
Occasional Paper 135; ISBN 0 255 36566 7; £7.50

Crime: Economic Incentives and Social Networks
Paul Ormerod
Hobart Paper 151; ISBN 0 255 36554 3; £10.00

The Road to Serfdom *with* **The Intellectuals and Socialism**
Friedrich A. Hayek
Occasional Paper 136; ISBN 0 255 36576 4; £10.00

Money and Asset Prices in Boom and Bust
Tim Congdon
Hobart Paper 152; ISBN 0 255 36570 5; £10.00

The Dangers of Bus Re-regulation
and Other Perspectives on Markets in Transport
John Hibbs et al.
Occasional Paper 137; ISBN 0 255 36572 1; £10.00

The New Rural Economy
Change, Dynamism and Government Policy
Berkeley Hill et al.
Occasional Paper 138; ISBN 0 255 36546 2; £15.00

The Benefits of Tax Competition
Richard Teather
Hobart Paper 153; ISBN 0 255 36569 1; £12.50

Wheels of Fortune
Self-funding Infrastructure and the Free Market Case for a Land Tax
Fred Harrison
Hobart Paper 154; ISBN 0 255 36589 6; £12.50

Were 364 Economists All Wrong?
Edited by Philip Booth
Readings 60; ISBN 978 0 255 36588 8; £10.00

Europe After the 'No' Votes
Mapping a New Economic Path
Patrick A. Messerlin
Occasional Paper 139; ISBN 978 0 255 36580 2; £10.00

The Railways, the Market and the Government
John Hibbs et al.
Readings 61; ISBN 978 0 255 36567 3; £12.50

Corruption: The World's Big C
Cases, Causes, Consequences, Cures
Ian Senior
Research Monograph 61; ISBN 978 0 255 36571 0; £12.50

Choice and the End of Social Housing
Peter King
Hobart Paper 155; ISBN 978 0 255 36568 0; £10.00

Sir Humphrey's Legacy
Facing Up to the Cost of Public Sector Pensions
Neil Record
Hobart Paper 156; ISBN 978 0 255 36578 9; £10.00

The Economics of Law
Cento Veljanovski
Second edition
Hobart Paper 157; ISBN 978 0 255 36561 1; £12.50

Living with Leviathan
Public Spending, Taxes and Economic Performance
David B. Smith
Hobart Paper 158; ISBN 978 0 255 36579 6; £12.50

The Vote Motive
Gordon Tullock
New edition
Hobart Paperback 33; ISBN 978 0 255 36577 2; £10.00

Waging the War of Ideas
John Blundell
Third edition
Occasional Paper 131; ISBN 978 0 255 36606 9; £12.50

The War Between the State and the Family
How Government Divides and Impoverishes
Patricia Morgan
Hobart Paper 159; ISBN 978 0 255 36596 3; £10.00

Capitalism – A Condensed Version
Arthur Seldon
Occasional Paper 140; ISBN 978 0 255 36598 7; £7.50

Catholic Social Teaching and the Market Economy
Edited by Philip Booth
Hobart Paperback 34; ISBN 978 0 255 36581 9; £15.00

Adam Smith – A Primer
Eamonn Butler
Occasional Paper 141; ISBN 978 0 255 36608 3; £7.50

Happiness, Economics and Public Policy
Helen Johns & Paul Ormerod
Research Monograph 62; ISBN 978 0 255 36600 7; £10.00

They Meant Well
Government Project Disasters
D. R. Myddelton
Hobart Paper 160; ISBN 978 0 255 36601 4; £12.50

Rescuing Social Capital from Social Democracy
John Meadowcroft & Mark Pennington
Hobart Paper 161; ISBN 978 0 255 36592 5; £10.00

Paths to Property
Approaches to Institutional Change in International Development
Karol Boudreaux & Paul Dragos Aligica
Hobart Paper 162; ISBN 978 0 255 36582 6; £10.00

Prohibitions
Edited by John Meadowcroft
Hobart Paperback 35; ISBN 978 0 255 36585 7; £15.00

Trade Policy, New Century
The WTO, FTAs and Asia Rising
Razeen Sally
Hobart Paper 163; ISBN 978 0 255 36544 4; £12.50

Sixty Years On – Who Cares for the NHS?
Helen Evans
Research Monograph 63; ISBN 978 0 255 36611 3; £10.00

Taming Leviathan
Waging the War of Ideas Around the World
Edited by Colleen Dyble
Occasional Paper 142; ISBN 978 0 255 36607 6; £12.50

The Legal Foundations of Free Markets
Edited by Stephen F. Copp
Hobart Paperback 36; ISBN 978 0 255 36591 8; £15.00